THE
FALLINGWATER
COOKBOOK

Elsie Henderson and a Daffodil Cake enrobed in whipped cream with strawberries in the Fallingwater kitchen. Photograph by Rob Long.

THE FALLINGWATER COOKBOOK

Elsie Henderson's Recipes and Memories

by SUZANNE MARTINSON
with JANE CITRON and ROBERT SENDALL

UNIVERSITY OF PITTSBURGH PRESS

A John D. S. and Aida C. Truxall Book

Published by the University of Pittsburgh Press, Pittsburgh PA 15260

Manufactured in Canada

Printed on acid-free paper

10   9   8   7   6   5   4   3   2   1

LIBRARY OF CONGRESS CATALOGING-IN-PUBLICATION DATA

Martinson, Suzanne.

   The Fallingwater cookbook : Elsie Henderson's recipes and memories /
by Suzanne Martinson ; with Jane Citron and Robert Sendall.

        p.   cm.

   Includes index.

   ISBN 13: 978-0-8229-4357-0 (cloth : alk. paper)

   ISBN 10: 0-8229-4357-3 (cloth : alk. paper)

   1. Cookery.   2. Menus.   3. Henderson, Elsie, 1913–   .   4. Kaufmann
family.   5. Fallingwater (Pa.)   I. Citron, Jane, d. 2006.   II. Sendall,
Robert.   III. Title.

   TX714.M3748   2008

   641.5—dc22

   2008019427

Suzanne Martinson dedicates this book to:

My mother, Ann Garner, an avid newspaper reader who read everything I ever wrote and only let slip one time that she thought something I wrote was "boring."

My late farmer father, Waldo M. Garner, a storyteller *par excellence* who never met an ice cream parlor he didn't like.

My husband, Bob "Ace" Martinson, who improves everything I write and makes me feel good about my work and myself, though there are foods he just won't eat.

Our daughter, Jessica, who from the first time she pulled up a wooden chair to help me make chocolate mousse, has been willing to taste any food.

Chef Robert Sendall dedicates this book to:
My mentor in the kitchen, my grandmother, Louise Weber, and my dear friend and collaborator, the late Jane Citron.

CONTENTS

PREFACE

In 1991, I was working as food editor and writer for the *Pittsburgh Press* when I interviewed Elsie Henderson for a newspaper story. Elsie had been the longtime (and last) cook at Fallingwater, the famous house Frank Lloyd Wright had designed for the Kaufmann family. As we cooks might say, everything jelled between us. Elsie and I became fast friends, although we couldn't have come from more different backgrounds. Our common bond was our love of good food and of Fallingwater.

The Kaufmann family hired Elsie in 1947. In her fifteen years there, first working for Edgar and Liliane Kaufmann and later for their only child, Edgar J. Kaufmann jr. (he preferred that junior not be capitalized), she made their meals and vicariously shared their secret joys and pain. Through the years, each time Elsie and I talked, I came to see this mystical place and its people through her eyes.

I began to imagine a book about the life and food of Fallingwater. Lynda Waggoner, director of Fallingwater, had already asked Elsie to write down her recipes for a possible cookbook for the Western Pennsylvania Conservancy, and eventually that small notebook in Elsie's fine hand was passed on to me. Over the years, Elsie and I greatly expanded on the collection, one by one, as she remembered certain dishes. Like many African American cooks, Elsie relies on her excellent memory for the ingredients and preparation of most of her recipes. In our many years as friends, I have seldom seen her refer to a cookbook. In fact, one black woman of my acquaintance—Dorothy Smith, director of Penn State Cooperative Extension of Allegheny County for twenty-six years—says it was the common belief among many fine black cooks that if you needed a recipe, you weren't much of a cook. Elsie tends to agree. "The old cooks never measured—the amounts were right, but the measuring was all in their head."

Her own recipes began with a list of ingredients and the most minimal instructions. However, as a longtime editor, I knew most people needed more than that, so, together, she and I worked out more complete instructions with mixing directions, pan sizes, baking times, and tests for doneness. She and I double-checked the recipes many times, especially when I had questions as I tested them. I also added information and tips that I believed would help the cook.

Elsie had been responsible for Fallingwater's baking, as well as lunches, breakfasts, and side dishes for dinner. Because the butler cooked the meats and seafood, she had few recipes in that category. This is where Jane Citron and Bob Sendall came in.

I knew Jane Citron from the *Pittsburgh Press*, where she wrote the "A la Carte" column in the days when I first met Elsie. Jane had a way of writing recipes that took the most complicated dishes and helped readers succeed at making them at home.

About that same time, in the early 1990s, Robert Sendall began producing special events at Fallingwater, where his innovative food impressed Lynda Waggoner, now Fallingwater's director and vice president of the Western Pennsylvania Conservancy. Later I met Bob, who, it turned out, was teaching cooking classes with Jane in Pittsburgh. Seeing them in action was like watching film clips of George Burns and Gracie Allen trading quips or enjoying Emeril Lagasse interacting with his doting fans. They played off each other, and though their exchanges were light-hearted, this twosome was serious about food.

So in addition to Elsie's remembered memories from the Kaufmann days, we have included Jane and Bob's modern, upscale preparations, which are suitable for entertaining but can be made—thanks to reader-friendly recipes—by the home cook. Lynda also suggested including recipes from the Café at Fallingwater. I contacted then-chef Mary Anne Moreau, who provided several delicious additions to the book.

So here we are, together—Elsie, Jane, Bob, Mary Anne, and me, between the covers of a book about the food of Fallingwater then and now.

A longtime Oregon friend, Saralie Northam, both a good cook and a great editor, also read this book and asked for some additional clarifications. The authors are also grateful to the researchers and writers of several books about the career of Frank Lloyd Wright and the building of Fallingwater and Kentuck Knob.

■

Elsie has never stopped learning about the language of food. The fall she turned ninety-four, she enrolled in a French class for seniors at the University of Pittsburgh. Through the pushes and pulls of creating this cookbook, Elsie seldom lost her sense of humor. When I asked her recently how many people a dish would serve, she quipped, "Four Republicans, or six Democrats." I'll leave you to interpret that.

The Kaufmanns enjoyed the comforting food that Elsie Henderson prepared for them. And now so can we.

ACKNOWLEDGMENTS

Many thanks to Cynthia Miller, director of the University of Pittsburgh Press, who always believed in this cookbook and memoir of Fallingwater, and to Deborah Meade, managing editor, who asked all the right questions in her editing. Their patience is palpable.

Led by Lynda Waggoner, vice president of the Western Pennsylvania Conservancy and director of Fallingwater, the staff at the historic house were invaluable to me. Special thanks to Clinton Piper, Cara Armstrong, and Denise Miner, and the neighbors of Fallingwater who provided their special insights.

Writing can be a lonely work, so thanks to our friends, especially our former Swan Acres neighbors in Pittsburgh, who encouraged me every halting step to publication. Kudos belong to two wonderful writers' groups, Dr. Montgomery Culver's meetings at the University of Pittsburgh and the get-togethers with Cathy Zimmerman from the *Daily News* at her Longview, Washington, home.

Thanks to Chef Robert Sendall, who creates food that looks as good as it tastes, for his food styling for Rob Long's photographs.

Gratitude is due to photographer Linda Mitzel, who turned over her kitchen to me and enlisted the patience of her family for a wild three days creating the photographs of Elsie Henderson's recipes.

Thanks to the industrious, creative farmers of western Pennsylvania and beyond. They inspired me throughout these pages.

Never underestimate the support of the staffs of six great newspapers: the *Champaign-Urbana (Illinois) Courier, Gresham (Oregon) Outlook, Daily News of Longview (Washington), Knoxville News-Sentinel, Pittsburgh Press,* and *Pittsburgh Post-Gazette.* We few formed a multitude, and we couldn't have done it without our loyal readers.

THE
FALLINGWATER
COOKBOOK

Fallingwater's black walnut dining table with ancient peasant chairs from Italy. Photograph by Rob Long.

ELSIE HENDERSON AND THE KAUFMANN FAMILY

Elsie Redmon (later Elsie Lee, then Elsie Henderson) was born at home in Pittsburgh on September 7, 1913. She is the youngest of thirteen children—eleven boys and two girls. Her father died when she was two. Her mother, Ada Redmon, cleaned houses and taught Elsie to bake with her own little utensils. Other than a cooking class at the Red Cross and French language lessons (the better to understand classic cuisine) at the downtown YWCA, Elsie has had no formal culinary training.

Elsie grew up on Pittsburgh's Mount Washington, which overlooks downtown's Golden Triangle, where the Monongahela and Allegheny Rivers meet to form the Ohio. "From our back bedroom, we could see downtown," Elsie remembers. Her large family lived in one three-room apartment plus a second apartment with four rooms. Sandwiched in the apartment between the Redmons was a woman who was so bent over that she paid Elsie a dollar a week, a princely sum in the 1920s, to scrub her bathroom floor. Perhaps it was that job that inspired Elsie to later spurn housekeeping as a career.

She inherited most of her childhood clothes from a wealthy family. "Their daughter would wear a dress two or three times, and then it was mine," she recalls. "I guess that's where I got my obsession with fashionable clothes." To shop for something special, she and her mother would hike down a road that ended at a streetcar tunnel not far from the Monongahela Incline, which carried paying customers up and down the steep Mount Washington. Then they walked across the bridge. Elsie recalls shopping at a favorite place, Lewin-Neiman Department Store, for a new dress when she was six or seven. It was the first time she remembers being racially stereotyped. The white saleswoman showed Elsie and her mother dress after dress, but she didn't see one that she liked. Eventually, her mother spotted one that appealed.

"Why didn't you show us that one?" her mother asked.

"I don't think you can afford it," the clerk said.

Her mother replied: "I've got eleven boys who work, and I can afford any dress in this place!"

By the time we met, Elsie was often the best-dressed woman in the room and, as she put it, "the poor woman's Imelda Marcos" of shoe lovers. Only imported Italian shoes will do for Elsie. Her sense of style starts with her appearance and encompasses her apartment and the food she creates.

When she was growing up, rich people on Mount Washington went to Elsie's mother when they had things that needed doing. The energetic Mrs. Redmon had taught herself to read and write and could do almost anything for her brood. But she told her boys, who had more formal education, that they'd have to be the ones to teach their eager little sister. At the age of five, Elsie had a library card. A year later, she walked, alone, a mile and a half from her hillside home to the Carnegie Library on Mount Washington's Grandview Avenue, which overlooks the city. "I didn't play with other children," she recalls. "The kids in the neighborhood had not a book in the house."

Elsie's elocution and handwriting have always been excellent. "When I skipped second grade, the teacher at Cargo Elementary School called in my mother to find out where exactly I learned to read," Elsie remembers. "From her brothers," her mother said.

"That girl always has a book," a worried neighbor told her mother.

"Pay no attention," Elsie's mother told her inquisitive daughter. "There's only one person like you and that's you."

Elsie comes from a line of strong females but grew up in a time when black women had few options in education or careers. She had planned to be a Licensed Practical Nurse until she discovered she was more comfortable with her hands in brioche than bandages. Her mother was born in the South, and some of the family recipes reflect this regional food, with its cornbread stuffing and sweet potato pie.

Elsie was a good student, but she was in a hurry to make money and so quit Pittsburgh's Schenley High School before she was graduated. Her first brush with the Kaufmann's Department Store family came when she was seventeen

Elsie Henderson in her Pittsburgh apartment with a 1964 Mary Shaw Mahrohnic charcoal portrait of herself. Photograph by Linda Mitzel.

years old. She was working at Kaufmann's Service Center when she saw her future boss, though at the time she didn't know who Edgar J. Kaufmann was.

For a young woman just out of high school, working in the store's bad accounts department had its share of guilty pleasures. "I always used to find the names of a number of people I knew who were delinquent paying their bills," she recalls. One of them was the boss's brother, Oliver Kaufmann. When he came by, Elsie teased him about not paying his bill. "I'll need a raise before I can afford to do that," he joked right back.

Her cooking career came next—working for families in the Borough of Sewickley Heights, an affluent neighborhood north of Pittsburgh. That experience led her to a white woman Elsie knew only as "Miss Gouzie," who linked wealthy Pittsburghers with servants. The woman introduced Elsie to H. J. "Jack" Heinz II, who was looking for a cook for Rosemont Farms, the Heinz estate in Fox Chapel, a wealthy borough north of Pittsburgh. She got the job, even though (or maybe because) she usually spoke her mind with her employers. "I was raised with eleven boys, and I got gumption," she says, quickly adding that she always knew how far to go when talking to rich people. She recalls: "Jack Heinz was right about one thing. He told me, 'Never pay attention to a recipe.'" Elsie seldom met a recipe she didn't change.

Through the years, she kept in touch with U.S. Senator John Heinz, son of Jack Heinz. She called him "Johnny" and remembers him as a mischievous, happy little boy playing with his dog. On one visit to Pittsburgh, he picked her out of a crowd and insisted on introducing her to Richard Thornburgh, the Republican governor of Pennsylvania (1978–1986). The governor, she says wryly, "certainly didn't want to meet *me*."

Twice married, with the corresponding name changes, Elsie is tight-lipped about those ups and downs in her life.

She enjoys talking, however, about her ongoing aspirations to culinary excellence. She uses the phrase Cuisine au Courant to describe her expertise after a lifetime of learning about trends in food and entertaining (and to grace her return address labels). Elsie avidly reads food magazines, such as *Bon Appetit*, and when I wrote and edited the food sections of the *Pittsburgh Press* and later the *Pittsburgh Post-Gazette*, Elsie always had questions and comments.

When she looked at cookbooks, such as the classic *Joy of Cooking* or *Flavor of France*, written by mother-daughter team Narcisse and Narcissa Chamberlain, she used them as inspiration, then struck out on her own to add, subtract, and revise—with one exception. "I tried to remain true to my mother's recipes," she says.

Most modern conveniences are anathema to Elsie. She treasures her Mixmaster and her dishwasher but has never used a food processor or a microwave—"I don't want anything in my kitchen I don't understand," she says. She has neither a cable for her television nor an answering machine for her telephone. Computer? Ha!

If Elsie listed every Pittsburgh notable she has cooked for in forty-plus years, it would read like a Who's Who of the city. The list of out-of-towners even includes the cookbook-writing Chamberlains.

About the only time Elsie ventured farther east than New York was for a summer in Hyannisport, Massachusetts. In 1965, Elsie worked for Eunice Kennedy Shriver, sister of Senator Edward Kennedy and the late president John F. Kennedy, while Mrs. Shriver's French chef was on vacation. During her summer there, Elsie recalls, ten-year-old Maria Shriver was on a diet—she was limited to three lamb chops—and Caroline and John Kennedy Jr. were "some of the best-behaved children I've ever seen." One summer day, when Senator Kennedy ventured out to the kitchen to ask what was for dinner, Elsie showed him some beef she had ground up from the roast she'd served the night before. Eunice, thinking frugally, had told Elsie to use up the meat. "I don't eat anything that's been ground up," Elsie remembers Ted Kennedy saying. Although he never ate any of her food, when Senator Kennedy visited Pittsburgh in 1983, he noticed Elsie in the crowd and, calling her by name, asked when she was coming back to Hyannis.

Despite the famous people she met over the years, Elsie's inspiration remains her mother, who looms largest in her memories. Her mother gave birth to all her children at home. "She was only in the hospital once in her life. She went in for cataract surgery and died there." Mrs. Redmon had an undiagnosed heart problem.

Edgar Kaufmann Sr., who knew Mrs. Redmon through Elsie, occasionally went missing from his downtown office in Kaufmann's. Eluding even his bodyguard, he would turn up at Elsie's mother's apartment in Terrace Village, a public housing development. He'd sit at Mrs. Redmon's kitchen table for hours, exchanging stories and enjoying her company. And her food. "He knew Mother's baking days," Elsie says with a grin.

■

To find Edgar Sr. sitting in Pittsburgh across the table from Elsie's mother, you have to trace his family history back across the years and miles to Germany. In 1869, Isaac Kaufmann joined his brother Jacob, who had immigrated to Pennsylvania from Hesse-Darmstadt. The brothers peddled clothes through the farms, villages, and coalfields in the Youghiogheny River Valley (interestingly, *Kaufmann* is German for merchant). Their sixty-mile route along the Baltimore and Ohio Railroad included Bear Run.

Isaac and Jacob Kaufmann opened a clothing store on Pittsburgh's South

Side in 1871, which they moved to a larger space nearby one year later. Their brothers Henry and Morris soon joined the enterprise, and the Kaufmanns added a second store on what is now Pittsburgh's North Side. In 1878, the brothers closed those two locations in favor of one large store in downtown Pittsburgh, at Fifth Avenue and Smithfield Street, where Kaufmann's Department Store, now a Macy's, still stands.

Edgar Jonas Kaufmann was born in 1885 to Morris and his wife, Betty, and Lillian Sarah Kaufmann (she later changed the spelling of her first name to Liliane), his future wife, was the daughter of Isaac, which made them first cousins. They married in 1909 in New York, because first cousins were not allowed to wed in Pennsylvania. Their son, Edgar J. Kaufmann jr., was born in Pittsburgh in 1910. He attended prep school at Pittsburgh's Shady Side Academy, though he left one credit shy of graduation. He studied painting in Europe, including Vienna, Florence, and London, and became a noted art collector, historian, and teacher.

Edgar Sr. bought Henry Kaufmann's share of Kaufmann's Department Store in 1913, and then he bought Isaac's. His uncle Jacob had died in 1905. Under Edgar and Liliane's leadership, business boomed, and Kaufmann's was named the most beautiful department store in America.

■

The Kaufmann and Redmon families came together when Elsie began cooking weekend meals—preparing breakfast, lunch, and side dishes for dinner—at Fallingwater in 1947. Elsie had answered a newspaper advertisement for a job she remembers thinking was "too good to be true." She interviewed for the position in the Kaufmanns' penthouse apartment, and accepted the offer, even though she was unsure about the job at first because it entailed traveling so far from the city each weekend. It did not take long for Elsie to fall in love with the work and the home beside the waterfall.

Fallingwater is a house in the trees, its music provided by a rushing mountain stream called Bear Run. It's not true that Frank Lloyd Wright dismissed this kitchen as simply "work space," as he had labeled some other kitchens in houses he designed. Yet by modern-day standards, the 15-by-12-foot room was nothing special: a Frigidaire when that name was synonymous with refrigerator, a Formica-topped kitchen table and four chairs, a bank of yellow metal St. Charles cupboards (the best at the time), and a stainless steel double sink. But a kitchen with a view like this is every cook's dream.

On her very first day, Elsie got an eyeful. It was 1947. She was thirty-three

The Kaufmanns: Edgar Sr., Edgar jr.,
and Liliane on the Fallingwater terrace.
Photograph courtesy of Western
Pennsylvania Conservancy.

years old. That day, she heard laughter and looked outside to see the Kaufmanns
and their guests as they splashed and frolicked in the chilly waters. Nude.

"I was standing there at the stove, and there were ten or twelve people—all
buck naked—under the falls. It was a mixed crowd, and some of them were on
their backs. I thought, 'It's a nudist camp!'

"What have I gotten myself into?" she wondered.

What she had gotten into turned out to be the highlight of her culinary career. She was there to cook for the rich and famous of western Pennsylvania and beyond—from violinist Isaac Stern to food magnate H. J. Heinz II—and she couldn't beat the view.

Elsie's preparation for Fallingwater weekends began on Thursdays when she checked with the Kaufmanns' weekday cook at their apartment in downtown Pittsburgh. She wanted to make sure she wouldn't cook the same foods for the weekend that the city cook had prepared during the week. Every Friday, the Kaufmanns' chauffeur, Harold Jones, picked up Elsie in Pittsburgh to drive her to Fallingwater, as she had never learned to drive a car. Early in her career, she sometimes took the streetcar or the bus to jobs, but most often she lived with her employers. At Fallingwater, she had her own room in the servants' quarters, upstairs in the guesthouse, and she started each day early. Sometimes the Kaufmanns traveled abroad or stayed at their designer home in Palm Springs, California. Elsie was paid whether she was called to Fallingwater or not.

Elsie, who has cooked for many wealthy families, classifies employers as those "who could keep help and those who couldn't." The Kaufmanns could. "Who could have guessed that I could ever call a place like Fallingwater home?" she says. "It was the best job I ever had."

BUILDING FALLINGWATER

The Breakfast Recipes

Frank Lloyd Wright imagined a country house that had more than just a view of a waterfall. He wanted the cascading stream to be part of it. His breathtaking design revitalized the architect's career and forever changed our ideas on merging place and space.

Completed with its service wing in 1939, the house was Fallingwater. Long before the American Institute of Architects named Wright's masterpiece the Building of the Century, it was the ultimate weekend getaway for a Pittsburgh department store family. The home was a fortuitous meeting of minds—a genius like Wright and daring patrons like Edgar and Liliane Kaufmann. Their little "country house" in southwestern Pennsylvania still inspires awe.

■

In 1916, Kaufmann's Department Store leased a Masonic country club at Bear Run to use as a summer camp for its female employees, according to Franklin Toker's *Fallingwater Rising*. The Kaufmanns built a modest summer cabin on the property in 1921, and the store bought the camp land in 1926.

It's little wonder the Bear Run air tasted so sweet. (It still does.) It was seventy-two miles from the smokestacks of the steel city, where business people changed their white shirts at midday because of the filthy air. The Kaufmanns called their cabin The Hangover, and it was rumored that the eggs were scrambled with vodka the morning after their parties.

The department store's women employees, and later men, were treated to a week of camp for $7, staying in cottages just above where Fallingwater would be built. They got off the train at the Bear Run station and walked the two miles up to the camp.

The late Earl Friend, who worked for the Kaufmanns and later the Western Pennsylvania Conservancy off and on for more than sixty years, remembered crowds of employees getting off the train. "It seemed like a hundred girls from the store . . . would come up every two weeks. They had sleeping cottages and fixed their eats at a big clubhouse." After lumbering fizzled in the 1920s, the people living near the Bear Run station moved on, and the railroad renamed the stop "Kaufmann."

The campers' food came from the area, and a special treat were the wild huckleberries, blackberries, and strawberries the camp cook bought from Joan Ream Cleaver's mother. Alverta Stull Ream and her brothers and sisters picked wild berries in the thickets and filled up big metal buckets. She received a quarter a bucket.

During the Depression, it was harder for the clerks to come up with the $7-a-week charge, so the camp was discontinued and became a private family camp for the Kaufmanns. About that same time, in 1934, Edgar jr., then twenty-five, returned to Pittsburgh after studying art in Europe. He signed on as an apprentice to Frank Lloyd Wright at Taliesin, near Spring Green, Wisconsin. Though Edgar jr. never intended to be an architect himself, he believed Wright was the world-class designer his family should hire for their new weekend home.

Wright was sixty-eight years old when the Kaufmanns commissioned the house in 1935. The site on which they would build was located in Fayette County, a two-hour train ride southeast from Pittsburgh, and just ten miles from the spot where President George Washington ambushed the French in 1754 in an opening salvo of the French and Indian War. The location had a view of Bear Run's forty-foot waterfall, and the Kaufmanns were surprised when Wright wanted to build the house cantilevered above the creek. "You love that waterfall," said the flamboyant architect, as he later recalled the conversation. "You should be close to it, a part of it." Besides, the location gave the house a pleasing southern exposure, a hallmark of Wright homes when the site made it possible.

Stories that Wright drew up Fallingwater's long-overdue plans in a day after Edgar Sr. announced a surprise visit have survived—and thrived. The architect was probably neither the first nor the last to procrastinate when an important project loomed. This one changed his life.

The architect and two Taliesin apprentices supervised the construction, which was done with local labor. Built deep in the woods in the depth of the Great Depression, Fallingwater was a complex structure built with men and horses. It seemed an impossible task.

Earl Friend was among the group of young men hired to build the house at 25 cents an hour, good wages during the Great Depression. One morning, ten minutes before starting time, Edgar J. Kaufmann appeared.

"Hey, somebody pick up this lumber and stack it over there," Edgar Sr. called out, pointing to a pile of boards. Earl hurried over to do the job.

"Give that man a raise to thirty cents," Edgar Sr. said. "He's the only one who cares about his work."

"I felt kind of funny getting that nickel raise when the others didn't, but I was glad to get it," said Mr. Friend, who died in 2007.

Following Wright's tradition of using local materials for his buildings, the stones were selected from the property and dragged to the site on sleds by two teams of Clydesdales. Bill Scarlett, whose father dug ditches, poured cement, quarried stone, and carried it to the stonemasons, watched the unconventional house go up. "It didn't look like much of a house to me," he said.

The Kaufmanns would come down on the weekends. While the crew was working on the scaffold around the outside of the first floor, workers spotted Edgar and Liliane under the falls, taking a shower.

It took a year to complete the main house and another year to finish the interiors. The guest house was completed soon after. When it was completed, the house's three dramatic levels seemed to spring from the rugged sandstone on the banks. Its massive fireplace, the centerpiece of the living/dining area, is built upon an outcropping of native rock that Wright incorporated into the hearth. The entrance hall, narrow and lined with stone, opens to a spacious room with a wall of windows that invites nature inside, a mural of green or gold or white depending on the season. A stairway in the main room leads down to the stream. The home's four terraces are integral to Wright's vision of an outdoor lifestyle among the rhododendron, hemlock, and oak.

When Fallingwater was finished, the Kaufmanns invited their neighbors to a party. For the locals, the construction had provided much-needed jobs, but they also knew that the Kaufmanns' big stone and concrete house was unique, its design rooted in the beauty of the place they called home. Earl Friend was at the housewarming. He remembered that they had hot wine in the big kettle hanging at the fireplace. "Some of these country women thought it was hot tea, so they got it, and then didn't know what to do with it!"

Once the house was built, the Kaufmanns retreated to Fallingwater to entertain guests in front of a crackling fire in the massive rock fireplace, to fish and swim in the bracing waters, and to dine on simple, delicious meals on the terrace. Not that their life in the woods was without comforts. Fallingwater had call buttons in the rooms so that the family and their guests could ring for maids dressed in custom-made uniforms. Every bathroom had an orchid, and the bars of soap were discarded after one weekend. A chauffeur stood by to drive. One man worked nearly full-time picking up errant leaves around the house and raking the driveway. A kitchen maid peeled green grapes for Liliane's favorite chicken salad.

Liliane and Edgar Kaufmann, the power couple that *Time* magazine in 1938 called "the merchant prince and princess of Pittsburgh," pampered themselves even when they were roughing it. Father and son hiked the hills around Fallingwater, but they had a masseuse to soothe their tired limbs. Liliane liked to fish, and her luck was good—her husband kept Bear Run, the stream that rushed under Fallingwater, well stocked with brown trout.

Concern for employees extended to the building of Fallingwater itself. Architect Wright once suggested that the Kaufmanns could save money by using less expensive materials in the servants' rooms. Edgar Sr. would have none of it. The same fine materials went into both. Not surprisingly, Fallingwater went well over budget. Wright estimated the house would cost $45,000. By the time the house and the guest/servant quarters were complete, the cost had risen to $150,000. And this was 1939.

Once the family moved in, there were a few changes to be made. Edgar jr. had studied with Wright and observed his sarcasm when his designs were questioned. The architect was more understanding when the family's needs fit into his vision. When the Kaufmanns requested additional storage for their books (Liliane was an avid reader, and Kaufmann's Department Store had an extensive book department), Wright added shelves in the stairway leading from the second to the third floor.

He approved the addition of a sitting room off the kitchen so the chauffeur and maids would have someplace to wait until they were called. There was never enough storage, so underneath the sitting room is a basement—its stairway is off the kitchen—for a refrigerator, toilet, and storage.

This stove, on display at Fallingwater, is similar to the original coal-burning Aga stove, which Edgar Sr. replaced for Elsie with a modern GE range. Photograph by Linda Mitzel.

Changes made to the kitchen itself demonstrated, in Elsie's opinion, how enlightened the Kaufmanns were. The original coal-burning Aga stove was a problem for someone who loved to bake as much as Elsie Henderson, because the temperature was hard to regulate. "You couldn't do fine baking in it," she says. At first, she baked some things at home in Pittsburgh so they'd turn out perfectly. That included the chocolate cake that her boss loved so much. But Edgar Sr. soon gave Elsie her choice of ranges, never mind the cost. "I got a new stove every three or four years. Most people work on the same stove all their lives."

Elsie notes that some wealthy employers saved money on food by having one menu for themselves and their guests, another for the hired help. One woman she worked for dumped leftover lobster from a lavish party into the disposal rather than giving it to the servants to enjoy. As the lobster disappeared down the drain, she stood by to make sure nobody snitched a taste. "Rich people are funny about food," Elsie says. Not so the Kaufmanns—their employees ate what they ate. "Most rich people are worried that you're going to steal from them," Elsie observes. "The Kaufmanns never even bothered to lock their liquor cabinet." In fact, the couple paid for the servants' twice-a-year parties at Fallingwater. Edgar Sr. was "always anxious to see what we thought of his wines," Elsie recalls. After one such party, when Liliane was leaving to catch a plane, she called to the servants on her way out, "What did you serve to drink?"

"On a scale of 1 to 10, I gave the Kaufmanns a 12," Elsie says.

The rosebuds came from Fallingwater's greenhouses, the Flowerpot Rolls with cinnamon sticks from Elsie's kitchen. Photograph by Linda Mitzel.

THE BREAKFAST RECIPES

There was no set time for breakfast at Fallingwater, although it was always served before 10 o'clock, and the Kaufmanns always walked afterward. The food was set out on the dining table for guests to enjoy whenever they awakened. When they appeared, they were asked how they like their eggs prepared, and the eggs would be made to order. Usually, there were home-baked breads, and visitors had a choice of coffee or tea, or a glass of rich whole milk from the farm's Jersey cows. The visitors might choose a sectioned grapefruit, fresh-squeezed orange juice, home-canned tomato juice, or select from a platter of fresh fruit.

CINNAMON-RAISIN COFFEE CAKE

This delicious yeast coffee cake is one of the breads the Kaufmanns enjoyed having for breakfast or serving to their guests. Breads like the Crescent Rolls (see recipe variation) were often served with butter and homemade preserves made by Jean Green, the wife of the head gardener, George Green. After the Greens were hired, the Kaufmanns built them a small house on the property. The husband was in charge of the gardens and the greenhouses, where he grew the fresh flowers and the vegetables for the table. In the off-season, produce was shipped in from all over the country by a Shadyside store. The woman proprietor kept the Kaufmanns' produce in the back, Elsie remembers, saving the absolute best for Falling-water. "She wouldn't even let the other clerks help me—she had to do it herself."

2 packages dry yeast

½ cup warm water (110 degrees F)

½ cup milk, scalded and cooled to lukewarm

½ cup butter, softened

½ cup granulated sugar

1 teaspoon salt

2 beaten eggs

4½ to 5 cups all-purpose flour

FILLING (FOR HALF OF THE DOUGH)

2 tablespoons butter, softened

½ cup light brown sugar

½ teaspoon cinnamon

¼ teaspoon nutmeg

1 cup finely chopped pecans

1 cup golden raisins

Additional butter, softened

In a small bowl, dissolve the yeast in warm water with a sprinkle of the sugar. The yeast should bubble after 5 minutes or so. Pour the yeast into a large bowl. Add the scalded milk to the softened butter, remaining sugar, salt, and eggs. Add the flour, a little at a time, until a soft dough forms. Work the dough by hand. Alternately, use an electric mixer.

Knead the dough on a lightly floured board, until it springs back to the touch. Place in a large greased bowl; cover with plastic wrap that has been sprayed with nonstick vegetable spray. Let the dough rise until double in bulk, about 2 hours.

To shape the coffee cake: Divide the dough in half. With a lightly floured rolling pin, roll the dough out into a rectangle about 9 by 24 inches.

Spread the rectangle with softened butter. Mix the brown sugar with the cinnamon and nutmeg. Add the chopped pecans and golden raisins. Crumble the mixture over the buttered dough.

Roll up, lengthwise, as for a jellyroll. Pinch the edge of the dough into the roll to secure.

Slice the roll into ¾-inch pieces. In a well-buttered tube pan, place the slices in circular layers. Overlap as needed. Cover and let rise until double in bulk.

Preheat the oven to 375 degrees F. Bake for 45 minutes, or until medium brown.

Repeat with the other half of dough, using the same amount of filling for the second batch, or you can make the other half into Crescent Rolls.

Serves 8 to 10

CRESCENT ROLLS: Divide the remaining dough in two. On a lightly floured board, roll each half into a circle ¼ to ½ inch thick. Spread the softened butter on the circle.

Cut the circle into eight triangles, as you would a pie. Roll up each triangle from wide to narrow end. Curve each roll to form a crescent, tucking in the pointed end. Brush with additional butter and let rise, until double. Bake in a 375-degree F oven, about 20 minutes. They will be light brown.

Makes 16 crescent rolls

Note: If the kitchen is cool, you can help the dough rise by putting a cup of water in the microwave. Bring the water to a rolling boil; turn off the microwave. Cover the dough and place it in the microwave with the steaming water.

CREAM PUFF BOWL

Not all the guests of the Kaufmanns made it to the dining table for breakfast. They could ring a maid to have a tray sent up to their room. Or they could dress and come downstairs. On some occasions, the morning food was a cream-puff "bowl," an eye-appealing way to

Cream Puff Bowl, filled with sausage, also can hold scrambled eggs or fresh fruit. Photograph by Linda Mitzel.

serve seasonal berries, peaches, nectarines, and citrus fruits, such as oranges and grape-fruit. In the winter, sliced bananas dipped into lemon juice joined a few frozen strawber-ries sweetened with a little sugar. On other occasions the "bowl" contained scrambled eggs surrounded with bacon, ham, or sausage.

1 cup hot water

½ cup butter

1 cup all-purpose flour

4 eggs, at room temperature

Confectioners' sugar for dusting, optional

Preheat the oven to 400 degrees F.

In a saucepan, heat the water to boiling. Add the butter and flour. Reduce the heat. Stir vigorously over low heat until the mixture forms a ball. Remove the pan from the heat and add eggs, one at a time, beating until smooth.

Spread the batter in the bottom of an 8- or 9-inch pie pan, which has been greased only on the bottom. Spread the batter on the bottom only, and, with the back of the spoon, make an indentation in the middle of the batter. Bake for 35 to 45 minutes, until nicely browned. When baked, cut a slit in the bottom of the "bowl" to let the steam escape.

Fill with cooked meats, creamed chicken, scrambled eggs, or fresh fruits. If us-ing fruit, dust "bowl" with optional confectioners' sugar. Omit if serving with savory foods.

Serves 4 to 6

FLOWERPOT ROLLS

Some guests at Fallingwater were introduced to a breakfast treat that they might never see anywhere else. One of cook Elsie Henderson's specialties was a cinnamon-infused sweet roll baked in a clay flowerpot. The night before, typically a Friday, Elsie mixed the dough and called the gardener to request eight perfect, tiny rosebuds from the greenhouse for the next day. She put a ball of dough into each small pot and inserted cinnamon sticks, let them rise, and baked them. Saturday morning, she arose early to reheat the rolls. When they were warm, she placed a rosebud in each cinnamon stick. One morning, a first-time guest confronted his flowerpot. Unbeknownst to him, "the other Elsie," Elsie Harbaugh, one of the housekeepers, watched from the third floor as he sat on the terrace below. He picked up the pot, turned it upside down, then right side up. Eventually the roll fell from its pot. By all accounts, the man enjoyed the roll. The rosebud lived to bloom another day.

Cure small flowerpots, which may be purchased at a hardware or garden store, by oiling them and then placing them in the oven at the lowest temperature for several hours.

In a large bowl, sprinkle the yeast over the warm water. Stir in the warm milk.

Add the sugar, salt, eggs, and soft butter; mix in about 2½ cups flour. Continue adding flour, a little at a time, until the dough is easy to handle. Alternately, make the dough with an electric mixer.

Work the dough on a lightly floured board until smooth and elastic.

Place the dough in a large buttered bowl and let it rise in a warm place, about 1 hour. It should double in size.

Butter the inside of each flowerpot. Shape dough into eight 2-inch balls and place one in each pot.

Brush the top of the dough lightly with softened butter. Insert 1 cinnamon stick into each dough ball. Cover the flowerpots with a towel and set them in a warm place. Let dough rise until double, or until the dough has reached the top of the flowerpots.

Bake at 375 degrees F about 10 to 15 minutes, or until lightly brown. Gently remove the rolls from their pot and place on a wire rack to cool slightly.

When ready to serve for breakfast, wrap the rolls in aluminum foil and heat in a 250-degree oven. Just before taking to the table, return the rolls to the flowerpots and place a small rosebud into each cinnamon stick.

Makes 8

Note: Although many old-fashioned recipes advise cooks to cover the dough with a "clean towel" (as if we'd use a dirty one), some bakers today prefer to coat plastic wrap with vegetable shortening spray (so it won't stick and cause the dough to deflate), then cover the dough with that. The translucent wrap makes it easier to check the dough's progress in rising.

8 small ceramic flowerpots, about 4 inches in diameter

1 package dry yeast

¼ cup lukewarm water (110 degrees F)

½ cup milk, scalded and cooled to lukewarm

½ cup sugar

1 teaspoon salt

2 eggs

½ cup soft butter

2½ cups all-purpose flour, or more

8 cinnamon sticks, with holes in center

Softened butter, for brushing the dough before baking

8 rosebuds

SOUR CREAM COFFEE CAKE

This streusel-topped coffee cake was a favorite for a light breakfast as a crunchy accompaniment to fresh fruit or berries. It's classified as a "quick bread," which means it doesn't require yeast, and it could be an impressive first project for a beginning baker.

¾ cup butter, softened

1⅓ cups granulated sugar

3 large eggs

1½ teaspoons vanilla

3 cups all-purpose flour

1½ teaspoons soda

¼ teaspoon salt

1½ teaspoons baking powder

1½ cups sour cream

STREUSEL TOPPING

1 cup light brown sugar, firmly packed

4 teaspoons cinnamon

1 cup chopped nuts (any kind)

4 tablespoons melted butter

CAKE: Butter a 9-by-13-inch cake pan.

Preheat the oven to 375 degrees F.

In the bowl of an electric mixer, beat on medium speed the ¾ cup butter, granulated sugar, eggs, and vanilla. In a separate bowl, mix the flour with the soda, salt, and baking powder. To the sugar and butter, mix in the dry ingredients, alternating with the sour cream. Beat until smooth. Spread the batter evenly in the prepared pan.

TOPPING: Mix the brown sugar, cinnamon, chopped nuts, and the 4 tablespoons melted butter. Evenly sprinkle the streusel over the batter to cover.

Bake in the preheated oven for 10 minutes; lower the temperature to 350 degrees, then bake an additional 20 to 30 minutes. The streusel topping should be brown.

Cut into squares to serve.

Makes 24 ample squares

Note: If using a dark pan, Elsie says, reduce temperature to 325 degrees F. Sour Cream Coffee Cake can also be baked in a Bundt pan. Pour half of the batter in Bundt pan, sprinkle with half of the streusel; repeat.

Sour Cream Coffee Cake, cut for breakfast, front, and Clove Cake, ready for dinner. Photograph by Linda Mitzel.

FRESH-FROM-THE-OVEN WALNUT MUFFINS

On Monday mornings, especially in the years when the Kaufmanns still raised lamb and milked dairy cattle on their Bear Run Farm, Edgar Kaufmann Sr. met with the outdoor staff to talk about the work they thought needed to be done in the next week. "We knew what had to be done, and we did it," said longtime employee Earl Friend. The crew gathered at Fallingwater to have a cup of coffee and a little breakfast snack. One favorite was these muffins made by Elsie Henderson and served warm with butter and homemade jam.

1 large egg

1 cup whole milk

¼ cup melted butter, or ¼ cup salad oil

¼ cup granulated sugar

2 cups all-purpose flour

3 teaspoons baking powder

1 teaspoon salt

1 cup walnuts, coarsely chopped

Preheat oven to 400 degrees F.

Butter 12 muffin cups.

In a bowl, beat together the egg, milk, butter or oil, and sugar.

Mix in the flour, which has been sifted together with the baking powder and salt. Allow the batter to be slightly lumpy. Fold in the nuts.

Fill the muffin cups two-thirds full of batter.

Bake for 20 to 25 minutes, or until brown. Remove from the pan immediately. Serve warm.

Makes 1 dozen muffins

Note: If you prefer to use muffin papers, place them in the muffin tins and lightly coat the papers with nonstick vegetable spray before filling. This prevents the muffins from sticking, making a more attractive presentation.

EGGS EN GELÉE

This was Edgar Kaufmann jr.'s favorite dish, which he also enjoyed for lunch. If he planned an early-morning hike, the eggs were prepared the night before and refrigerated. The fresh tarragon likely came from his mother's herb garden on the third-floor terrace. This dish was included in a poem that Elsie Henderson wrote about Fallingwater: "And aah— the food! Eggs en Gelée, Mourning Dove, Avocado Mousse, Pheasant Roast, Gazpacho, Chestnut Mountain, Whole Salmon Glazed on every fin and gill (foods we common folk have rarely heard of) served by a butler, no less…"

In a pan, cook the chicken wings in 2 to 3 cups water to cover (you will need at least 2 cups broth). Remove the wings from the liquid; discard the wings. Chill the broth. Skim off the fat.

To 2 cups of the cold broth, add the gelatin, salt, and soy sauce. Chill until slightly jelled. Cover the bottoms of 4 individual compotes (or custard dishes) with gelatin. Refrigerate. Allow to set. Refrigerate remaining gelatin.

After the broth has jelled, in a frying pan, lightly poach the eggs in a few table-spoons of water. The yolks must be soft. Chill.

Place the chilled poached egg atop the gelatin in the compotes, then cross two tarragon leaves on top of each poached egg. Set bowl of reserved gelatin in hot water until it reaches pouring consistency. Cover eggs with liquid gelatin. Set in the refrigerator to solidify.

Serve thoroughly chilled.

Makes 4 servings

Notes: When an egg is absolutely fresh, its yolk will sit tall and be centered in the white, and its thick white will take up more space than the thin white, making for a compact egg. An older egg will spread out in the pan. Today, fresh eggs are harder to come by, and the hen house where yours were laid may be several states away.

There are antidotes to less-than-fresh eggs. Using a cold egg will reduce how much the egg will "feather," or spread, in the pan. Or you can buy an egg poacher, either for the microwave or for the countertop. Egg rings are available, too.

When all else falls, an ill-shaped poached egg can be trimmed with a biscuit cutter to form the perfect circle befitting Eggs en Gelée.

Like any animal product, cooked eggs should be refrigerated.

6 to 8 chicken wings (about 1 pound)

1 tablespoon unflavored Knox gelatin

¼ teaspoon salt

Few drops soy sauce

4 poached eggs

2 fresh tarragon leaves per egg

Elsie's Scones with dried cranberries and a drizzle of frosting. Photograph by Linda Mitzel.

SCONES

Among the many guests Elsie Henderson remembers baking for were two from Bucking-
ham Palace, the equerry and lady-in-waiting to King George VI and Queen Mother Eliz-
abeth. The lady was heard to remark, "We don't get this kind of service at the palace!"
These scones made them feel quite at home. At Fallingwater, scones were served warm
with butter and homemade jams made with local berries.

Preheat the oven to 450 degrees F.

Sift the flour, baking powder, and salt into a bowl.

Cut in the chilled butter with a pastry blender or two knives. Add the cream and milk, which have been combined. Stir in the liquid with a fork until the dough comes away from the side of the bowl.

On a lightly floured surface, roll out the dough into a square ½ inch thick. Cut into quarters. Cut each square in half, forming two triangles. This will yield eight scones.

Bake in the preheated oven. Depending on the size of the triangles, scones will bake in 12 to 15 minutes. They will be light brown on top, with white sides.

Makes 8 scones

VARIATIONS: Add ½ cup dried cranberries, raisins, chopped apricots, or toasted pecans. The grated rind of 1 large orange may also be added to the dough. The orange rind is nice in combination with dried cherries. Some bakers like to add white chocolate.

Note: The recipe can be doubled, and the squares for making the triangular scones may be cut larger or smaller, depending on preference.

3 cups all-purpose flour

2 teaspoons baking powder

1 teaspoon salt

⅓ cup butter, chilled

¼ cup cream

½ cup whole milk

EGGS BENEDICT

The Kaufmanns had eclectic tastes when it came to guests. The senior Kaufmanns were host to scientist Albert Einstein, opera singer Richard Tucker, and Raymond Loewey, the "father of industrial design," who was connected to projects as diverse as NASA space-craft, the Greyhound bus, the Lucky Strike package, and a line of Frigidaire refrigerators and freezers. Elsie says that after Loewey's visit to Fallingwater, he returned to his home outside Paris, which had belonged to Henry IV of France. Eggs Benedict are a classic breakfast dish to serve, no matter who the diners may be.

HOLLANDAISE SAUCE

6 egg yolks

2 tablespoons lemon juice

1 teaspoon salt

3 to 4 drops Tabasco sauce

1 cup melted butter

EGGS

6 thick slices Canadian bacon
or lean ham

6 eggs

3 English muffins, split and toasted

HOLLANDAISE SAUCE: In a blender or bowl, mix the egg yolks, lemon juice, salt, and Tabasco. Slowly pour in the melted butter and mix on low speed.

EGGS: Sauté the meat in a bit of butter. Poach the eggs; keep warm.

Place 1 slice ham on each English muffin half; top with a poached egg. Spoon the warm Hollandaise over all.

Serves 6

Note: To poach the eggs, in a deep sauté pan, bring enough water to cover the eggs to a boil; add a little vinegar and salt. Reduce the heat to barely simmering (a few bubbles should come to the top). Crack each egg in turn onto a saucer and slip the eggs, one at a time, into the gently bubbling water. Simmer for 3 minutes for a medium-firm yolk, adjusting time up to 5 minutes for a solid yolk.

LIFE AT FALLINGWATER WITH LILIANE AND EDGAR KAUFMANN SR.

The Lunch Recipes

For wealthy people in the 1950s, "home cooking" meant a cook who lived in. Well-traveled people like the Kaufmanns knew that the best food was made with fresh ingredients prepared from scratch. Elsie found an appreciative family at Fallingwater.

When Liliane Kaufmann married her first cousin, she and Edgar formed a formidable couple, if not always a contented one. If Liliane had an eye for beautiful clothes, furnishings, and art, her husband shared that, plus an eye for women. "He was the biggest playboy in Pittsburgh," Elsie says, then amends, "Make that the Western world." The Kaufmanns had separate bedrooms, but at the time that was common among wealthy couples, especially ones as unconventional as they were. Liliane had the master bedroom, and her husband had a single bed in the room next door, which their son referred to as his father's "dressing room."

Liliane was a career woman who took great pride in her boutique, the Vendome Shops, on the eleventh floor of Kaufmann's Department Store. Pittsburgh women didn't need to travel to New York or Los Angeles as long as Liliane was selecting cutting-edge fashions, antiques, and art. Her eye for style was impeccable, and she traveled to Paris to make sure her shop had all the latest looks. Kaufmann's carried many sculptures and home furnishings, some of which ended up at Fallingwater. She sometimes clashed with Frank Lloyd Wright, who, not content to simply design the Kaufmanns' country house, wanted to control how it was furnished, too. The dining table he designed seated six people, though an extension could be attached to create seating for thirteen. He imagined diners sitting in his barrel chairs. Liliane Kaufmann had something else in mind: a group of three-legged peasant chairs that she'd purchased in Italy. Her son took her side. In Edgar jr.'s *Fallingwater: A Frank Lloyd Wright Country House,* there is a picture of the "sample" barrel chair, which was relegated to the upstairs guest room. He wrote, "the slender barrel chair Wright proposed . . . seemed static, when grouped, and was not adopted." The chairs chosen by his mother "added liveliness." They also worked better on the uneven stone floor.

Fallingwater was Liliane Kaufmann's place to let loose, to entertain artists, to read, to escape. Avant-garde with an artistic eye, she was an able businesswoman, too, a woman who knew what she wanted, though she didn't always get it, particularly when it came to her fractious marriage. She loved her son and her show dogs—six long-haired dachshunds, to be exact.

Elsie, who never says anything bad about either the parents or their son, recalls that when Liliane left for Pittsburgh, she kissed the dogs that were staying behind in the country. The country dogs were chauffeured to town for farewell kisses if Liliane was traveling to California or Mexico.

Liliane's dogs ate meat, and only the best meat. The deliveryman bragged that he delivered beef for the Kaufmanns, not realizing it was for the dachshunds. "I was told that during the war years someone told Mrs. Kaufmann it was sinful to feed the dogs Grade A meat when most people were rationed," Elsie remembers. Liliane replied, "I don't give a damn. My dogs didn't start the war!" On weekends, it fell to Elsie to prepare the dogs' bacon and eggs for breakfast. She'd fry a pound and a half of bacon until it was dry, and then scramble a dozen eggs. "I crumbled the bacon up in them. The plates went up to Mrs. Kaufmann's room, so she could watch them eat." On Friday nights, the dogs dined on whitefish poached in milk. Elsie came to have her own affection for the animals. And if Edgar Sr. didn't love his wife's dachshunds, he acted as if he did.

Liliane, who had attended finishing school near Philadelphia, made frequent trips to New York and Europe. She had high standards when it came to food, though she wasn't an eager eater herself. When she had company, Liliane joined her guests and ate what was prepared. When it was just the family, however, she might have only a slice of fresh fruit, some julienne vegetables, and a couple of pieces of cheese. She was as beautiful and slim as a model and a walking, talking advertisement for the designer fashions at the Vendome. Moreover, she expected others to show the same restraint when it came to eating. "She didn't want any heavy people around her," Elsie recalls.

She enjoyed her margaritas and Chesterfield cigarettes. Though she hated to cook, she loved mixing up unusual concoctions for the Cherokee red cast-iron kettle, which could be swung into the massive fireplace to heat grog for her guests. There was one small problem. "It took eight hours to heat," Elsie says, so the staff usually heated the drink in the kitchen and then poured it into the kettle.

Among the guests who gathered around the kettle were the late Bill Block, the publisher of the *Pittsburgh Post-Gazette*, and his wife, Maxine, who spent a weekend there. Mr. Block, who was more than six feet tall, remembered ceilings that were low and furniture that was uncomfortable. "How about a nice swim after breakfast?" Liliane Kaufmann asked the couple. Knowing his hostess's penchant for swimming in the nude, Mr. Block, always the gentleman but a man with a wry sense of humor, said, "Thanks for asking, but I think we'll just take a nice walk in the woods."

The Kaufmanns were more flexible than other rich families Elsie had worked for. They didn't measure every move or orchestrate every menu. Liliane knocked before she entered the kitchen, but she made her presence known. She had several sets of dinnerware and never liked to use the same service twice in a weekend. She didn't care what went on the table, Elsie says, "just so they were different."

To plan her menus, Elsie kept meticulous notes of what the Fallingwater guests were served, so they wouldn't have the same meal on later visits. Fallingwater residents received the same treatment. Avoiding duplication for Liliane's evening snack was especially challenging in the winter. Elsie arranged a fruit plate that was delivered to Liliane's bed stand—in the 1940s, few fruits were available out of season. If a plate had apples one night, they were off-limits the next. "If Mrs. Kaufmann was hungry for something, we'd have it flown in, no matter what it cost," Elsie recalls. Fallingwater's yearly food budget was never less than $30,000.

Only the best was good enough. The Irish linen sheets cost $350 a dozen and required the laundress to have an apt hand with an iron. The towels, also in medium beige, were Wamsutta. The built-in closets had pullout shelves with wicker bottoms so the linens could air properly. The house, Liliane told friends, could be damp.

Liliane sometimes traveled to Mexico alone, and when she was not at Fallingwater, her husband would invite people she didn't like. When the maid told Edgar Sr. that a female guest's things had been put in Edgar jr.'s room on the third floor, he said, eyes twinkling, "Thank you, Florence. At least we'll start out that way."

If there was solitude for Liliane Kaufmann in the forests around Fallingwater, there could be loneliness, too. She counted on her maid for companionship. "Florence is the only one who listens to me," she often said. Florence (her last name is lost to memory) wore beautiful, custom-made, silk uniforms. Like most people in the fashion industry, Liliane took great stock in a person's appearance, and that extended to her staff. Elsie's previous employers had wanted her to buy her own uniforms, but Liliane had her come in for a personal fitting. Four uniforms were sewn, and they cost $350, a small fortune in 1947. Liliane herself dressed informally at Fallingwater, wearing walking shorts and sandals or colorful floral dresses she'd purchased in Mexico.

When the Pennsylvania weather turned warm, the meals were moved to the terrace. Elsie will never forget the sight and sound of one informal luncheon there. Liliane, who helped the Sisters of Mercy at their hospital during World War II, had invited a table full of nuns. Dressed in their habits, wimples and veils, the eight sisters had a grand time. "I could hear them chattering and laughing all the way into the kitchen," Elsie remembers.

Liliane's passion for health-related causes extended far beyond having the sisters to lunch. The spectrum of her service to two Pittsburgh hospitals went from wrapping bandages to plotting policy. In 1942, she trained at Georgetown Hospital in Washington for the Red Cross Nurse's Aid Corps and took on a full-time job at Mercy Hospital in Pittsburgh helping regular nurses in the emergency department. She volunteered at the hospital for ten years, serving on committees and representing it at Pittsburgh's Council of Medical Social Service. This was a task she was well equipped to handle. In 1934 she had been

A Picasso over the nightstand, and three choices of fruit such as Elsie might have set out for Liliane's bedtime snack. Photograph by Linda Mitzel.

membered a visit from the inquisitive millionaire, who had dark wavy hair and a scar that ran from eye to nose, the result, as the story went, of a youthful saber fight in Germany. One day, her mother, Goldie Hay, who was reared on land that's now part of the Western Pennsylvania Conservancy, was baking bread. She didn't have enough bread pans, so balls of dough were rising all over the house. The little girl was mesmerized as she watched the city man trade stories with her father, Lloyd Hay. Edgar Sr. did not come calling in city suits. He wore shorts and big, heavy shoes that came up above the ankles. His knee socks, ringed in red and gray, didn't cover his hairy legs. "He had a little old tree that he carried as a walking stick," Mrs. Dull recalled. "He sat in our old Mom Johnson rocking chair. Every time he rocked, it squeaked. We kids were kind of embarrassed and giggled over that."

Edgar Sr. knew the country way of helping neighbors. When the local dairy farmers worried about prices, Kaufmann joined them in organizing the Mountain Top Co-op, as Virginia Friend Kessler, daughter of local farmer Sturgis Colborn, explains. She remembers Edgar Sr. at the co-op's banquet. "The ladies of the church cooked a delicious meal, and I remember this fantastic dessert—a round ice cream with cherries all over the top. See, we didn't have things like that." When the co-op lost its bottler, Edgar Sr. approached the Hagan Dairy Company in Uniontown, which had unintended consequences for local architecture. Kaufmann suggested to owners I. N. Hagan and his wife, Bernardine, that Frank Lloyd Wright was just the man to design a house on land they owned near Ohiopyle. They hired Wright, who designed Kentuck Knob, and that made the Hagans and Kaufmanns neighbors. The Hagans sometimes dropped by, "usually around lunch," Elsie recalls, and they were always invited to stay: "I guess they liked the food at Fallingwater."

Edgar Sr.'s graciousness with people extended to his staff. Butler Phillip Carter, who cooked the meats and served the various courses, always dressed in a white coat and dark pants, although it could get hot and sticky on the terraces in the summer. Phillip recalled one day when he was serving lunch to Edgar Sr. and what he called several of Pittsburgh's "captains of industry." A former dancer, Phillip was light on his feet and he described himself as a big, hefty guy, though "always neat and well-kept." His forehead was beaded with sweat as he removed one course and brought another. "When I brought Mr. Kaufmann his entrée, he quickly took his handkerchief out of his breast pocket and patted my forehead with it," Phillip recalled. "He gave me a big smile and a wink as he did it, too."

Edgar jr. studied in Florence with Viennese artist Victor Hammer, who painted this portrait of Edgar Sr., here with Elsie Henderson. Photograph by Linda Mitzel.

Phillip cringed at being known as a "butler—what does it mean to *butle*, anyway?" he joked not long before his death. If he sometimes thought of himself as much a friend to the Kaufmanns as a servant, it's understandable. When his mother became ill, the Kaufmanns added a bathroom to the first floor of a house on the property so that she could live close by to her son. "Mrs. Kaufmann always told me to 'make a little extra' so Phillip could take a plate to her," Elsie recalls.

Elsie also remembers a second chauffeur, a black man from the South, who saved if she had been taken to a hospital nearer Fallingwater, rather than driven to Pittsburgh.

After Liliane's untimely death, Edgar Sr. married Grace Stoops in 1954. He died seven months later, in Palm Springs, before he ever got to ride in either the Rolls or the helicopter. Elsie was too upset to attend the funeral. The second Mrs. Kaufmann died not long after that.

Yet when Elsie remembers the Kaufmanns, she smiles to think of all the good times. She enjoyed not only the beauty of the home, but the characters of the people who lived there, despite—or because of—their eccentricities. One of Edgar Sr.'s quirks was his difficulty sleeping and resulting penchant for roaming around the house at all hours. Though the refrigerator shelves were often filled to overflowing, Elsie was careful to save a spot for him. He knew a midnight snack awaited.

Some nights Elsie left a slice of Red Devil's Food Cake on the kitchen table, where the two of them had started their day at Fallingwater, together.

Caraway Twists, Cinnamon Rolls, and Corn Sticks atop the Aga stove. Photograph by Linda Mitzel.

THE LUNCH RECIPES

Lunch at Fallingwater was served precisely at one o'clock. It was presented in the French style, with soup first, then the main course, followed by salad. The dessert was served at the table, too. Depending on the menu, the plates for each course were either chilled or heated.

Liliane didn't make a big deal out of it, but when the butler was serving, she surreptitiously tested the platter with her forefinger to make sure it was hot.

Frank Lloyd Wright enjoyed Elsie's Crab Salad when he ate lunch at Fallingwater in 1956. Photograph by Linda Mitzel.

SALADS, SOUPS, AND ONE-POT MAIN DISHES

THE WRIGHT CRAB SALAD

In the fifteen years Elsie Henderson cooked at Fallingwater, she prepared only one meal for architect Frank Lloyd Wright, who died in 1959 at age 92.

Edgar Kaufmann jr., who had inherited Fallingwater from his parents, asked the architect to come from Taliesin West in Arizona to set the house right after it flooded in 1956.

Elsie and the chauffeur picked up the architect at the Pittsburgh airport. Although they might have saved time by taking Interstate 376 in downtown Pittsburgh, Wright asked to be driven through the city's Oakland-Shadyside area, where four colleges are clustered. He especially wanted to see the University of Pittsburgh's forty-two-story Cathedral of Learning on Fifth Avenue.

"It's the tallest Keep Off the Grass sign I've ever seen," Wright said, as they drove past the monumental structure. "They had to build it up," Elsie tried to tell the architect. "There wasn't enough land to do anything else."

A pen-and-ink drawing of Elsie from that time pictures her as a woman of beauty. Her appearance prompted Frank Lloyd Wright to say, "If you cook as well as you look, everything is all right."

After Frank Lloyd Wright talked to the workmen about flood repairs, he ate a simple repast of Crab Salad and Corn Sticks with lemon sherbet for dessert. He sat alone at the black walnut veneer table he had designed for Fallingwater's dining area.

Rinse the crabmeat well and remove any shell fragments. Pat the crab with paper towels to remove excess moisture. Mix the crab gently with the celery and peppers, taking care not to break it into shreds. Moisten the mixture with salad dressing. Do not overdress.

Serve on Bibb lettuce leaves.

Serves 4

Note: It is important to buy lump crabmeat, although the back fin crab may be less expensive. The Kaufmanns' crabmeat usually came from the Chesapeake Bay.

2 pounds lump crabmeat, picked over

½ cup heart of celery, finely chopped

½ medium red pepper, finely chopped (about ¼ cup)

½ medium green pepper, finely chopped (about ¼ cup)

Boiled Salad Dressing (recipe on page 53)

Bibb lettuce leaves, washed and patted dry

CHEESE SOUFFLÉ

Cheese Soufflé was Edgar Sr.'s top-of-the-list luncheon favorite. For guests, tomato sauce was served over the soufflé, or sometimes mushroom sauce. Edgar Sr. preferred strawberry preserves. Cook Elsie Henderson was proud of this dish. "There was almost as much soufflé above the pan as in it."

THICK CREAM SAUCE

4 tablespoons butter

4 tablespoons all-purpose flour

1¾ cups whole milk

Dash salt and pepper

Pinch of nutmeg

SOUFFLÉ

¾ cup grated cheese (a combination of Swiss cheese and Parmesan)

6 eggs, separated (reserve 1 yolk for another use)

CREAM SAUCE: In a saucepan on low heat, combine the butter and flour. Add the milk. Simmer the sauce, stirring constantly, until it thickens. Sauce will be very thick. Add the salt, pepper, and nutmeg.

Stir the cheese into the hot sauce. Remove the pan from the heat, let cool, and add 5 beaten egg yolks, stirring constantly. Cool.

SOUFFLÉ: In a glass bowl or the metal bowl of an electric mixer, beat the 6 egg whites until stiff but not dry. Stiff peaks will form.

Carefully fold one-third of the beaten whites into the cooled cream sauce. When well distributed, very lightly fold in the rest of the egg white mixture.

Make an aluminum foil collar for a 2- to 2½-quart soufflé dish. Pour the mixture into a soufflé dish, or straight-sided casserole. Place the dish in a hot water bath (see note) and bake in a 375-degree F oven for about 45 minutes, or until high and browned. Serve immediately.

Note: Here's how to prepare a hot water bath, also called a Bain-Marie. Once the soufflé mixture has been poured into the soufflé dish, place it in a large pan that has been filled with boiling—or very hot—water. This method assures uniform baking of the delicate soufflé.

Serves 3 to 6

H. J. HEINZ CORN CHOWDER

When Fallingwater was built, commercially canned soups were readily available—for a dime. That didn't mean that the wealthy families of Pittsburgh fired their cooks and opened a can. Elsie Henderson quickly learned that when she applied for a job as cook for H. J. "Jack" Heinz II.

"Do you know how to make good homemade soup?" she was asked.

"Of course," she replied, "but the H. J. Heinz Co. makes all kinds of soups."

"Yes, but those are for the public, not for the family."

Later, when Elsie was cooking for the Kaufmanns, Jack Heinz was invited to lunch. Edgar Sr. asked her to make something his guest was especially fond of. She made corn chowder. Homemade, of course.

At the table, Heinz tasted the soup and nodded his approval to his host. "My cook used to make a soup like this," he said. Edgar clapped his hands, and his cook emerged from the kitchen.

"Elsie, it's you!" Heinz said. They all had a good laugh over that.

Fry the bacon in a sauté pan until it is very crisp and dry. Pour the drippings from the pan, reserving ½ tablespoon or more. Chop the bacon into small pieces.

To the drippings, add the celery and onion, and cook until tender. Blend in the flour and then the milk, stirring constantly until smooth.

In a saucepan, cook the potatoes in water to cover until they are tender. Drain.

To the milk mixture, add the creamed corn and the potatoes. Stir in the bacon.

Sprinkle with fresh chopped parsley and paprika.

Serves 4

Note: Liliane Kaufmann was particular about her corn, and this recipe is made her way. She insisted that after the ears were husked and washed and the corn silk was removed, only the tip of each kernel be cut from the cob with a sharp knife. The rest of the kernels left on the cob were discarded. Elsie placed the tender kernels in the oven on low heat to draw out the natural "cream" from the corn.

½ pound bacon

½ to 1 tablespoon bacon drippings

½ cup finely chopped celery

1 small onion, finely chopped

2 tablespoons flour

4 cups whole milk

2 cups cooked potatoes, peeled and well chopped

2 cups creamed corn (see note)

Fresh chopped parsley and paprika, for garnish

LAUREL HIGHLANDS GAZPACHO

Today, we would call the key ingredient in this Gazpacho "heirloom" tomatoes. The freshness of the cold soup, which was made from vegetables grown within miles of Fallingwater, made it Edgar jr.'s favorite lunch when he came in from New York for the weekend. He never learned to drive and he would travel by train from his Manhattan apartment, often with friends, and be met in Uniontown, Pennsylvania. The chauffeur would drive the party to Fallingwater.

3 cups tomato juice

2 beef bouillon cubes

2 fresh tomatoes, peeled, seeded, and chopped

½ teaspoon Tabasco sauce

1 teaspoon Worcestershire sauce

1 teaspoon salt

2 tablespoons pure olive oil (not extra virgin)

4 tablespoons red wine vinegar

¼ cup finely chopped onion

¼ cup chopped green pepper

½ cup chopped cucumber (do not pare)

Croutons, for garnish (directions follow)

The night before the Gazpacho is to be served, heat the tomato juice in a large soup pot. Add the bouillon cubes and heat until dissolved. Add all the remaining ingredients, except the croutons. Bring to a simmer. Remove from the heat.

Cool the Gazpacho to room temperature and chill overnight. At the same time, chill the soup bowls.

Serve the soup cold and topped with crisp croutons. To make the croutons: Cut day-old homestyle or Italian bread into bite-size squares. In a frying pan, sauté the cubes lightly in butter, a few at a time, until lightly browned on all sides. Remove from the pan. Cool on paper towels. Store in an airtight container.

Serves 6 to 8

Note: To easily peel the tomatoes, drop them, one by one, into boiling water for 10 to 20 seconds. Remove with metal tongs. The skins will slip right off.

Seasonal cucumbers and peppers for Laurel Highlands Gazpacho. Photograph by Linda Mitzel.

Borscht, made with fresh beets, with a dollop of sour cream.
Photograph by Linda Mitzel.

BORSCHT

Borscht was another one of Edgar jr.'s favorite lunchtime soups. He had studied in Europe, where this cold beet soup is a mainstay on some tables. In the summer, the ingredients would have been grown in western Pennsylvania. The components, of course, are readily available in winter, too.

4 cups chopped, cooked beets

1 quart beef broth

2 cups shredded cabbage

4 tablespoons minced onion

2 teaspoons granulated sugar

2 teaspoons fresh-squeezed lemon juice

Sour cream, for garnish

Wash 4 or 5 beets, remove the tops and root end, and submerge them in cold water in a soup pot. Bring the water to a boil, and simmer the beets until they are tender, or when a fork can easily be inserted into the center of each beet. Cool slightly and peel. Chop into pieces.

In a large pot, mix the broth with the beets, cabbage, onion, sugar, and lemon juice.

Bring the soup to the boiling point. Reduce the heat and simmer about 10 minutes. Cool.

Chill the soup thoroughly in the refrigerator for several hours or overnight. Meanwhile, chill the soup bowls.

Serve the chilled Borscht with a dollop of sour cream.

Serves 6 to 8

CORN PUDDING

Walks in the woods and dips in the plunge pool worked up an appetite, so guests were offered a wide array of food. Liliane Kaufmann enjoyed entertaining with a buffet on the terrace, anchored by cold meat platters (cooked fresh for the buffet, never left over from an earlier meal). A typical buffet might include thinly sliced baked ham, sliced chicken breast, Corn Pudding (recipe follows), mixed green salad with Boiled Dressing (recipe page 53), Elsie's Popovers (recipe page 58) and butter, sherbet, and Pecan Shortbread (recipe page 65).

At one rather elaborate buffet, suddenly all the electricity went off. The Kaufmanns immediately invited people to stay for dinner. One guest exclaimed: "We would be delighted to stay here, because we don't have this kind of food at my house!"

Preheat the oven to 350 degrees F. Butter a 1½-quart casserole.

Husk and rinse the corn on the cob, removing the corn silk. With a sharp knife, cut off the tips of the kernels into a bowl. Run the blunt side of the knife blade over the cob to extract the corn "milk." Discard the cobs, along with the partial kernels left intact.

Lightly whisk the yolks until well mixed. Mix in the sugar and salt.

Measure the cream in a glass cup, and whisk in the cornstarch. Mix into the corn-egg mixture.

Pour the mixture into the greased casserole. Sprinkle bread crumbs on top.

Bake for 25 to 30 minutes, until the mixture is set and the top is brown.

Serves 4

6 ears of corn (8, if small)

3 eggs yolks (save whites for another use)

2 tablespoons granulated sugar

Pinch salt

¼ cup cream

1 tablespoon cornstarch

Bread crumbs

EGG FU YUNG

For this luncheon specialty, the Fallingwater owners made a rare exception to Liliane Kaufmann's "no leftovers" rule. When there was leftover roast pork, the family enjoyed this Chinese-style dish. As always, the butler cooked the meat, while Elsie Henderson made the dishes cooked on top of the range or baked in the oven.

EGGS

3 tablespoons vegetable oil

6 eggs

1½ cups fresh bean sprouts, washed and drained

1½ cups finely chopped cooked pork, trimmed of fat

4 tablespoons chopped green onions, use white and a little of the green

2 tablespoons soy sauce

SAUCE

1 tablespoon cornstarch

1 tablespoon sugar

1 tablespoon white vinegar

3 tablespoons soy sauce

EGGS: In a large skillet, heat the vegetable oil.

In a large bowl, with a wire whisk, beat the eggs until thick and light. Stir in the bean sprouts and the cooked pork. Add the green onions and the 2 tablespoons soy sauce.

Pour one-third of the mixture into the heated oil. When slightly set, push the egg over, gently rolling it on itself until you have a cylinder, lightly browned all over. Repeat for the other two portions.

SAUCE: In a small pan, combine the cornstarch, sugar, vinegar, and the remaining 3 tablespoons of soy sauce. Cook, stirring constantly, until the mixture thickens and boils. Continue stirring until cornstarch is dissolved. Pour over the eggs.

Serves 3

Note: If fresh bean sprouts are not available, canned sprouts may be used, but they should be well drained, rinsed, and patted dry.

COUNTRY VICHYSSOISE

One of Liliane Kaufmann's joys in having a house in the country was growing her own fresh herbs for the meals that were served to her family and friends. It's easy to imagine her going out onto her sunny, third-floor terrace to snip some fresh, green chives for this soup. Liliane wasn't one to upbraid the staff or even to declare what her guests would be having for lunch. But that doesn't mean she was not paying close attention to details. "The Kaufmanns always said they 'hired good people and then let them do their jobs,'" Elsie Henderson says.

In a large saucepan, simmer the leeks, potatoes, and salt in Chicken Broth for 25 to 30 minutes, until the vegetables are soft and tender.

Working in small batches, put the soup through a blender; blending until smooth. Return the blended mixture to the large saucepan.

When all are blended, add the milk and cream. Mix well; chill thoroughly.

Before serving, sprinkle each bowl of cold soup with finely chopped chives.

Makes 8 to 10 luncheon servings

Note: Chill soup bowls in the Frigidaire (this is how Elsie always refers to the refrigerator) before filling.

12 chopped leeks, all the white with a little green

2 large potatoes, peeled and cubed (red potatoes cook faster)

Scant 2 teaspoons salt

6 cups Chicken Broth (recipe follows)

1 cup whole milk

1 cup light cream

Finely chopped chives, for garnish

CHICKEN BROTH

In addition to using the homemade broth as an ingredient in recipes, cook Elsie Henderson cooked baby vegetables—"Mrs. Kaufmann wanted no carrot larger than the size of her forefinger"—in the broth, adding a dash of sugar.

In a large soup pot, bring 4 quarts of water to a boil. Add chicken wings, celery, carrots, dry herbs, parsley, salt, pepper, and cayenne pepper. Bring to a boil. Reduce the heat and simmer for 2 hours, or more, adding additional water as necessary. Refrigerate the broth; the fat will rise to the top and solidify. Skim off the fat, which can be used for sautéing. Strain the broth and refrigerate in small containers.

Makes 4 quarts

Note: Leftover Chicken Broth may be frozen.

2 to 3 dozen chicken wings

2 or 3 stalks of celery

2 or 3 chopped carrots

Dry herbs to taste

Fresh parsley

Salt

Pepper

Pinch of cayenne pepper

QUICHE LORRAINE

Real men do eat quiche, especially one as delicious as this entrée, rich with meat, cheese, and cream. Liliane Kaufmann would have limited herself to a narrow sliver.

Pastry for deep-dish 9- or 10-inch pie (recipe page 96)

12 slices bacon or 12 link sausages, thinly sliced

1 cup shredded Swiss cheese

¼ cup minced onion

4 eggs, beaten slightly

2 cups light cream

¾ teaspoon salt

⅛ teaspoon cayenne pepper

Preheat the oven to 425 degrees F.

Crisply fry the bacon or sauté the sausages. Drain well. Crumble the bacon or drop the pieces of sliced sausage into the unbaked piecrust.

In a small bowl, mix the cheese, onion, eggs, cream, salt, and cayenne. Pour into the crust.

Bake for 15 minutes in the preheated 425-degree F oven. Reduce the heat to 300 degrees F and bake for 25 or 30 minutes longer. The quiche will be golden brown.

Let stand for 15 minutes before cutting. This gives the custard time to set up.

Serves 6 to 8

Note: To avoid overbaking the crust, fold a 2-inch wide strip of aluminum foil around the pie plate, encasing the edge of the pastry, before placing the quiche in the oven. Remove the foil for the last half of the baking time.

LAMB AND ROSEMARY CHILI

Without even thinking, when Elsie Henderson wrote out this recipe for this book, she wrote 1 teaspoon sucre, which is the French word for sugar. After seven-plus decades of reading recipes, she often slips into the language of that formidable cuisine. Around 1978, she undertook more formal language training when she was one of ten people who enrolled in French lessons at Pittsburgh's Downtown YWCA on Wood Street. When she turned ninety-four, she again took up the study of French in a class for seniors at the University of Pittsburgh.

In a large frying pan, cook and stir the ground lamb, onion, and rosemary until the meat is brown and the onion is tender. Season with the salt, white pepper, and chili powder. Add the tomato sauce, sugar, and white kidney beans.

Heat to boiling, reduce the heat and simmer, uncovered, about 1 hour, stirring occasionally, until of desired consistency.

Serves 3 as a luncheon main course

Note: Sometimes Elsie sautéed cubes of lamb roast for this dish. To use this method and double the recipe, use 2 pounds cubed lamb, ½ cup finely chopped onion, 1 tablespoon minced green pepper (omit rosemary), 1 tablespoon chili powder, 4 cups tomato sauce, 2 teaspoons sugar, salt and pepper, and 3 15-ounce cans of white beans, drained. Simmer until desired consistency and adjust seasoning.

1 pound ground lamb

1 yellow onion, finely chopped

¼ cup finely chopped fresh rosemary

1 teaspoon salt

¼ teaspoon white pepper

1½ teaspoons chili powder

1½ cups home-canned or commercial tomato sauce

1 teaspoon sucre (sugar)

1 large can (about 19 ounces) white kidney, or cannellini, beans

LAMB CURRY

Talk about from the farm to the table! When sheep grazed in the pastures of Bear Run Farm, tasty lamb chops were close to home. "When you came down the hill past the barn, you thought it had snowed, there were so many wooly, white lambs," Elsie recalls. In this recipe, she usually used the less expensive shoulder pieces, rather than leg of lamb, which Edgar Sr. shipped on Mondays to business associates and friends.

Heat the oil in a large saucepan. Sauté the onion and celery. Add the curry powder, salt, and flour; stir. Slowly add the chicken broth, stirring constantly. Cook until smooth and thickened.

In another pot, heat the olive oil and cook the lamb cubes, stirring frequently, until the meat is nicely browned on all sides and tender when pierced with a fork. Don't overcook; the cubes should be slightly pink inside.

Add the curry sauce and serve over hot rice.

Serves 3 to 4

Note: To cook rice, remember this formula: 1-2-1. It stands for 1 cup rice, 2 cups water, and 1 teaspoon salt. In a heavy saucepan, bring the water, rice, and salt to a boil, reduce heat, cover, and simmer for 20 minutes. Don't peek. Serves 3 to 4.

1 tablespoon vegetable oil

1 onion, finely chopped

½ cup celery, finely chopped

1 tablespoon curry powder

½ teaspoon salt

2 tablespoons flour

3½ cups Chicken Broth (recipe page 49)

2 tablespoons olive oil

2½ cups cubed lamb (from the shoulder or the leg)

Hot cooked rice

HAM AND CHEESE LUNCHEON CASSEROLE

This ham and cheese combo is perfect to pack into an insulated carrier and tote to a family or community potluck.

2 cups shredded sharp cheddar cheese

1 cup light cream

5 cups peeled, sliced potatoes, partially cooked

3 cups cubed cooked ham

4 tablespoons chopped pimiento

½ cup seasoned fine bread crumbs

Heat the oven to 350 degrees F.

In a large saucepan, heat the shredded cheese with light cream, stirring constantly, until the cheese is melted and the sauce is creamy. Remove from the heat.

Layer the sliced potatoes with the cooked ham in a greased, 2-quart casserole, or a 9-by-13-inch loaf pan. Pour the sauce over the layers and sprinkle with pimiento and seasoned bread crumbs. Cover. Bake 40 to 45 minutes. The top will be medium brown.

Serves 6 to 8

LILIANE KAUFMANN'S CHICKEN SALAD

When you hire a congenial staff, you can order about anything you'd like to eat. Liliane Kaufmann preferred peeled grapes in her chicken salad. "I didn't peel them," Elsie explains, "the kitchen maid peeled them." Though it seems hard to imagine, peeling grapes, a tedious job at best, really does put this chicken salad a notch above any other. The larger the grapes, the easier the job. The homemade Boiled Salad Dressing makes an immense difference, too.

⅔ cup Boiled Salad Dressing (recipe follows)

4 cups cooked chicken breast

2 teaspoons poultry seasoning

¼ teaspoon onion salt

Dash white pepper

¾ cup finely chopped celery

1 cup sliced water chestnuts, well drained

1 cup large seedless green grapes, peeled

Hearts of Bibb lettuce

In a frying pan, poach 4 or 5 chicken breasts in a little water. Simmer, covered, until done. To test, insert a knife in the thickest in part of the breast. The juice should run clear. Drain and cool the chicken. Bone the breasts and remove the skin. Cut into bite size pieces.

Mix together the Boiled Salad Dressing, seasonings, chicken, celery, water chestnuts, and peeled grapes. Serve at room temperature on hearts of Bibb lettuce.

Serves 8

BOILED SALAD DRESSING

The Kaufmanns did not eat commercial bottled dressings, so theirs were always made from scratch.

Mix the flour, sugar, salt, and dry mustard in a saucepan. In a small bowl, beat the egg yolks with the milk and vinegar. Stir the mixture slowly into the flour, whisking as you pour. Cook on the range over medium heat until the mixture is thick. Remove from the heat. Add the butter and stir. Cool to room temperature for serving. Cover and refrigerate the unused dressing.

Makes 2 cups

Note: Leftover dressing can be kept for approximately two weeks in the refrigerator.

¼ cup all-purpose flour

1½ teaspoons granulated sugar

½ teaspoon salt

1 teaspoon dry mustard

2 egg yolks

1½ cups whole milk

⅓ cup vinegar (either white or cider vinegar)

1 tablespoon unsalted butter, at room temperature

CREAMY CHICKEN CASSEROLE

This casserole is simplicity itself. It could be served with a mélange of fresh fruit and some piping hot popovers (see recipe page 58).

In a large frying pan, sauté the chopped onions in butter or chicken fat. Add the flour, salt, and pepper and stir until the onion is soft and translucent.

Add Chicken Broth and milk.

Heat the mixture to boiling, stirring constantly.

Add the water chestnuts and cooked chicken. Heat through.

Remove from the heat and add the sherry. Pour the mixture into a 9-by-9-inch buttered casserole.

Sprinkle with the buttered crumbs and place under the broiler until the crumbs are lightly browned.

Serves 6

2 cups cooked skinless, boneless chicken breast, coarsely chopped

½ cup butter or chicken fat

2 tablespoons chopped onion

½ cup all-purpose flour

1 teaspoon salt

½ teaspoon pepper

2 cups Chicken Broth (recipe page 49)

½ cup whole milk

1 cup whole water chestnuts, thickly sliced

4 tablespoons dry sherry (not cooking sherry)

1 scant cup buttered bread crumbs

CHICKEN AVOCADO CRANBERRY SALAD

Liliane Kaufmann often traveled to California and Mexico, where she grew to love avocado, which at the time might have been considered exotic by some Northeasterners, especially in rural areas such as southwestern Pennsylvania. Although avocados were first shipped to Chicago and New York in the 1920s, sales in the Midwest have risen only recently. As one early wholesaler said, "Nobody here wants black fruit." For any produce that was out of season or not available at farms near Fallingwater, the Kaufmanns had a standing-order account at a Shadyside market, where the family purchased many of their groceries. Elsie says she often featured avocado in salads when Edgar jr. and his companion Paul Mayen were at Fallingwater. "Mr. Mayen loved avocados."

6 cups cooked chicken breast, chilled and cubed

1 cup dried cranberries, soaked overnight, drained and patted dry

½ cup finely chopped celery

¼ teaspoon salt

¼ teaspoon white pepper

1 cup Boiled Salad Dressing (recipe page 53)

¼ cup finely chopped parsley

4 or 5 avocados, peeled, pitted and thickly sliced (see note)

In a large bowl, add the cranberries to the cooked chicken. Mix in the celery, salt, pepper, dressing, and chopped parsley.

To serve, arrange the salad on a large round serving plate.

Prepare the avocado at the last minute so it won't darken. Peel, pit, and thickly slice each avocado. Encircle the chicken salad in the center of the dish with the thick slices of avocado. Figure on one-half avocado per person.

Serves 8 to 10

Notes: Here's how to cut an avocado: With a sharp paring knife, peel the avocado. Holding the fruit in one hand, crosswise around its circumference, slice the fruit into crescents, from top to bottom, just until the knife hits the pit. If not serving immediately, squirt the slices with lemon juice to avoid discoloring.

Supermarket avocadoes are usually sold while still hard, so they should be purchased several days in advance. They are ripe when the skin yields when pressed gently with the thumb.

Chicken Avocado Cranberry Salad is an excellent recipe for a women's luncheon.
Photograph by Linda Mitzel.

AVOCADO MOUSSE

Elsie made this dish in a ring mold. But it can also be made in a round gelatin mold and presented on a pretty plate.

1 tablespoon Knox gelatin, softened in ¼ cup cold water

1 cup hot Chicken Broth (recipe page 49)

1 tablespoon lemon juice

1 teaspoon sugar

2 large avocadoes, peeled, pitted, and mashed

½ cup Boiled Salad Dressing (recipe page 53)

½ cup sour cream

½ teaspoon seasoning salt

Dash Tabasco

Bibb lettuce leaves

In a large bowl, add the hot Chicken Broth to the softened gelatin. Refrigerate. When the gelatin has thickened, remove from the refrigerator.

In a bowl, add the mashed avocado, lemon juice, sugar, dressing, sour cream, salt, and Tabasco to the gelatin. Mix well.

Pour the mixture into a 1-quart ring mold that has been rinsed with cold water.

When set, unmold the mousse on a few leaves of Bibb lettuce. If desired, the ring may be filled with shrimp salad.

Serves 6 to 8 as a side dish

Notes: To unmold gelatin, run a metal spatula around the edge of the set mixture. Dip the bottom of the ring into a bowl of hot water; removing after about 5 seconds. Invert the ring and let the mousse drop gently onto the serving plate.

Making gelatin is a reversible reaction. If the gelatin becomes too solid to add the avocado mixture, fill a large bowl with hot water. Dip the bottom of the bowl of gelatin into the water. Stirring constantly, allow the gelatin to become the right consistency. Likewise, if a gelatin mold becomes too soft, put it in the refrigerator and it will set up again. Freezing, however, ruins gelatin.

BREADS AND ROLLS

RYE FISH LOAF

Elsie Henderson, who has a playful sense of humor, liked to surprise her employers and their guests. One of her creations was a rye bread baked in the form of a fish, which she served alongside real fish, such as the brown trout caught fresh in Bear Run. For lunch, the butler would throw the trout on the grill, and when the fish was cooked, Elsie would lay the fishy bread beside the trout on the buffet table. The guests would point at her presentation and share a laugh.

Dissolve the yeast in the lukewarm water. Stir in the milk, sugar, eggs, butter, flours, and caraway seeds. In the large bowl of a stand mixer, work the ingredients until a sturdy dough is formed. The mixture should come away from the sides of the bowl to form a ball. Alternately, mix by hand with a wooden spoon.

On a lightly floured bread board, knead the dough until smooth, about 10 to 15 minutes. Small blisters will appear on the surface of the dough when the kneading is complete.

Place the dough in a large buttered bowl. Cover with a towel and let rise in a warm place until the dough doubles in size, about 1 hour in a warm kitchen; punch down.

Knead the dough and make into another ball. Shape into a cylinder and place in a well-buttered fish-shaped pan. Cover and let rise 25 minutes.

Bake in a 375-degree F oven for 25 to 35 minutes, until nicely brown. The fish will sound hollow when tapped.

Alternately, bake in two bread loaf pans.

Makes 1 large "fish" or two loaves

Note: At Fallingwater, a copper-colored metal 9-by-12-inch jumping fish pan was used for the rye bread.

1 package active dry yeast

¼ cup warm water (110 degrees F)

¾ cup lukewarm whole milk

¼ cup sugar

2 eggs, beaten

⅓ cup soft butter

3 cups unbleached all-purpose flour

1 cup rye flour

¼ cup caraway seeds

BLUEBERRY MUFFINS

In the countryside around Fallingwater, the energetic natives often hunted huckleberries, as wild blueberries are known, to pick and sell to Fallingwater cook Elsie Henderson. She liked to bake muffins, which might accompany a light lunch of soup or salad. In huckleberry season, the muffins found their way onto many a breakfast tray, too—although never on the same weekend that they were served for lunch.

1 egg

1 cup whole milk

¼ cup butter, melted, or ¼ cup vegetable oil

¼ cup granulated sugar

2 cups all-purpose flour

3 teaspoons baking powder

1 teaspoon salt

1 cup fresh huckleberries or frozen blueberries, patted dry

Preheat the oven to 400 degrees F.

Butter a 12-muffin pan or use muffin papers.

In a small bowl, with a wooden spoon, beat the egg, milk, melted butter or oil, and sugar. Set aside.

Sift the flour with the baking powder and salt into a large bowl. Make a depression in the dry ingredients and pour in the egg-milk mixture. Stir just until mixed. Do not beat. The batter will be slightly lumpy.

With a large spoon or spatula, fold in the fresh berries. If using frozen blueberries, thaw, and drain well, and pat dry before mixing into the batter.

Fill muffin cups two-thirds full.

Bake for 20 to 25 minutes, or until the tops are light brown. Remove from the pan immediately. Serve warm or at room temperature.

Makes 1 dozen

ELSIE'S POPOVERS

Don't be intimidated by popovers. With a little practice, these amazing, eggy rolls can be mastered. Popovers contain no leavening agent, such as baking powder or yeast, because they are steam-leavened. Keep the oven door closed, especially during the first 20 minutes or so.

4 large eggs

2 cups whole milk

2 cups sifted all-purpose flour

1 teaspoon salt

Preheat the oven to 450 degrees F.

Spray a 12-muffin pan with oil or grease with butter. (If the oversized, heavy pans manufactured especially for popovers are used, the recipe will make 9.)

In a bowl, blend the eggs, milk, flour, and salt with either a hand mixer or a whisk just until smooth. Do not overbeat, or they won't pop.

Fill the muffin cups about half full.

Bake in the preheated oven for 25 minutes, then lower the heat to 350 degrees F and bake 15 minutes more.

The popovers should be nicely browned. After removing them from the oven, prick each popover with the tip of a sharp knife to allow the steam to escape.

Makes 12

VARIATION: For Cheese Popovers, add ½ cup shredded sharp cheddar to the batter.

CORN STICKS

Elsie loved the old-fashioned cast-iron corn stick pans that are popular in the South—so many memories, such crunchy crust. These are a nicely textured accompaniment for scrambled eggs or a luncheon salad. They may be served with butter or jam or just eaten plain.

Preheat the oven to 450 degrees F. Butter the metal corn stick pan(s) and preheat in the oven. Alternately, use heavy muffin pans or a well-greased cast-iron skillet.

In a bowl, mix the cornmeal, flour, baking powder, sugar, salt, and soda. Add the buttermilk and eggs. Mix thoroughly, and add the melted butter. Stir until well blended.

Fill the pans. The recipe will make enough batter for three pans, each with seven 5-inch corn sticks.

Bake 15 minutes, or until nicely browned. The preheated pans give a crispy crust.

Makes 21 corn sticks

Notes: Stone-ground cornmeal adds extra crunch to these sticks.

The cast-iron corn stick pans Elsie uses are available at hardware and cooking stores, as well as in some catalogues.

1½ cups yellow cornmeal

½ cup all-purpose flour

3 teaspoons baking powder

1 teaspoon sugar

1 teaspoon salt

½ teaspoon baking soda

1½ cups buttermilk

2 eggs, lightly beaten

⅓ cup butter, melted

DESSERTS

MINT CHOCOLATE ANGEL FOOD CAKE

Elsie includes this cake recipe, which appeared in Gourmet *magazine, in remembrance of the late U.S. Senator John Heinz (R-Pennsylvania). Elsie cooked for his divorced father when the senator was a boy, and he was spending the summer on Rosemont Farms near Pittsburgh. This was the precocious five-year-old's favorite cake.*

1 cup cake flour (not self-rising)

½ cup unsweetened cocoa powder

½ teaspoon salt, divided

1½ cups superfine granulated sugar, divided

10 eggs, separated (reserve yolks for another use)

1½ teaspoons cream of tartar

⅔ teaspoon peppermint extract

Preheat the oven to 375 degrees F.

Into a bowl, sift the flour, cocoa, ¼ teaspoon of the salt, and ¼ cup of the sugar.

In a large metal or glass bowl of an electric mixer, beat the egg whites until they are foamy; add the cream of tartar and the remaining salt. Beat in the remaining sugar, a little at a time, continuing until the whites form soft peaks.

Gently fold in the mint extract and the flour mixture, ¼ cup at a time.

Pour the batter into an ungreased 14-by-10-inch tube pan with a removable bottom, and run a knife through the batter to remove any air bubbles.

Bake the cake in the middle of the preheated oven for 35 to 40 minutes, or until a tester comes out clean; invert the pan on the work surface, and let the cake cool completely in the pan. Run a thin knife around the edge of the pan to separate the side of the cake. Run the knife under the bottom of the cake and around the tube to loosen the cake and invert the cake onto a plate.

Serves 10 to 12

Notes: Never use a plastic bowl to beat egg whites. Plastic absorbs miniscule globules of fat, which prevent the egg whites from achieving the maximum volume. The mixing bowl and the beaters should be meticulously clean for the same reason.

When beating egg whites, stop the mixer and lay the flat side of a metal spoon on top of the beaten whites. Lift the spoon gently. A "soft peak" will topple. Stiffly beaten egg whites will have peaks that stand upright.

Pennsylvania apples picked
especially for Fruit Crisp.
Photograph by Linda Mitzel.

FRUIT CRISP

*Fresh produce was abundant in western Pennsylvania, and it often became the centerpiece
of meals at Fallingwater. To the Kaufmanns, a simple plate of fruit was dessert. For those
who like their fruit embellished, this dessert is another comforting example of the good living with good food.*

8 cups fruit (peaches or apples)

½ cup brown sugar

½ cup granulated sugar

1 cup quick oatmeal

1 cup all-purpose flour

1 teaspoon vanilla

1 teaspoon cinnamon

Dash nutmeg

1 cup melted butter

Cinnamon Whipped Cream
(directions follow)

FRUIT CRISP: Preheat the oven to 375 degrees F.

Butter a 9-by-12-inch baking dish. Spread the peeled and sliced fruit over the bottom of the dish.

In a small bowl, mix the sugars, oatmeal, flour, vanilla, cinnamon, nutmeg, and melted butter. Stir with a fork until well combined.

Sprinkle over the fruit.

Bake in the preheated oven for 30 to 35 minutes. The topping will be brown.

Serve warm with Cinnamon Whipped Cream.

CINNAMON WHIPPED CREAM: Whip 1 cup extra-heavy cream. Sweeten with about ¼ cup confectioners' sugar and fold in ¼ teaspoon cinnamon.

Serves 12 to 18

SWEET DROP DUMPLINGS

Alverta Stull Ream, who grew up on the land near Fallingwater, liked to use her home-canned wild berries from the Bear Run area in this delectable dessert, so rich and sweet the dumplings are practically a meal in themselves. Bisquick, a time-saving mix popular with the home cook, was invented in 1930.

1 quart canned huckleberries or blackberries, with juice

1 cup granulated sugar

2 cups buttermilk baking mix (Bisquick or other brand)

¼ cup sugar

⅔ to 1 cup whole milk

Cream for topping

In a pot with a cover, add the 1 cup sugar to the berries and boil until the sugar is dissolved and the mixture thickens slightly.

In a bowl, combine the baking mix, milk, and the ¼ cup sugar with a fork. The dough will be soft. Drop by tablespoons in circles atop the boiling berries. Leave a space in the center, as the dumplings will double in size. Reduce the heat to simmer; cook for 10 minutes. Cover the pot and simmer for an additional 10 minutes.

Top with rich milk or cream and serve warm.

Makes 10 to 12 dumplings

JERSEY ICE CREAM

This vanilla custard ice cream has a creamy color and the richest of textures because of the cream and the egg yolks. Until 1952 when the herd was sold at auction, the milk came from the Kaufmanns' registered Jerseys, the breed made famous by Elsie the Borden Cow.

Separate the eggs, reserving the egg whites for another use. (For example, see recipe for Mint Chocolate Angel Food Cake, page 60.)

In a heavy saucepan, combine the sugar, salt, and whole milk. Cook on the range over medium heat, stirring until the sugar dissolves and the mixture is hot, 6 to 8 minutes.

In a small bowl, whisk the egg yolks. Gradually whisk in about 1 cup of the warm milk mixture. Return the egg mixture to the saucepan, reduce the heat to medium low and cook, stirring, until the custard thickens enough to coat the back of a metal spoon, about 5 to 10 minutes.

Let cool for 1 hour at room temperature. Stir in the vanilla and cream.

Refrigerate until very cold, about 6 hours, or overnight.

Pour the custard into the canister of an ice cream maker and freeze according to manufacturer's directions. Use about 6 parts ice to 1 part rock salt for freezing.

For soft-serve ice cream, serve immediately. For hard ice cream, transfer to a covered container and freeze at least 3 hours, or as long as three days.

Serves 6 to 8

Note: Elsie says she usually doubled this recipe.

4 egg yolks, at room temperature

1 cup granulated sugar

½ teaspoon salt

2 cups whole milk

2 tablespoons vanilla

4 cups extra-heavy cream

PENNSYLVANIA PEACH ICE CREAM

After a bracing morning hike in the Laurel Highlands, nothing could beat a fresh peach grown in the area. Unless, of course, it would be a bowl of this peach ice cream. A tasty accompaniment is Pecan Shortbread cookies (recipe page 65).

8 egg yolks, at room temperature

2 cups granulated sugar

¾ teaspoon salt

4 cups whole milk

2 teaspoons vanilla

6 cups extra-heavy whipping cream

4 cups ripe peaches, peeled and pitted

1 cup granulated sugar

1 teaspoon vanilla

Separate the eggs, saving the whites for another use.

In a heavy saucepan, combine the sugar, salt, and whole milk. Cook over medium heat, stirring until the sugar dissolves and the mixture is hot, 6 to 8 minutes.

In a bowl, whisk the egg yolks. Gradually whisk in about 2 cups of the warm milk mixture. Return the egg mixture to the saucepan, reduce the heat to medium low and cook, stirring, until the custard thickens enough to coat the back of a spoon, about 5 to 10 minutes.

Let the mixture cool 1 hour at room temperature. Stir in the 2 teaspoons vanilla and the cream.

Slice the peaches, then cut into thirds. In a blender or food processor, chop the peaches until they are small chunks. Do NOT puree. Add the 1 cup sugar and the remaining 1 teaspoon vanilla to peaches and any juice. Add the peach-sugar mixture to the cooled custard.

Refrigerate until very cold, about 6 hours, or overnight.

Pour the custard into a canister of a large ice cream maker and freeze according to the manufacturer's directions. Use about 6 parts ice to 1 part rock salt for freezing.

For soft-serve ice cream, serve immediately. For hard ice cream, transfer to a covered container and freeze at least 3 hours or as long as three days.

Serves 12 to 16

VARIATION: For Bear Run Strawberry Ice Cream: Substitute 2 pints (4 cups) chopped strawberries for the peaches.

Note: Eggs that are cold are easier to separate into yolks and whites. Let the eggs come to room temperature before cooking or baking with them. This is especially important when working with egg whites, which reach greater volume when beaten to peaks for meringues or cakes.

PECAN SHORTBREAD

Preheat the oven to 350 degrees F.

In the bowl of an electric mixer, cream the butter and add confectioners' sugar. Sift flour with the baking powder and salt. Stir into butter-sugar mixture.

Work the pecans into the dough with your hands.

On a lightly floured board, roll out the dough into a rectangle ⅓ inch thick.

With a sharp knife, cut dough into 2½-inch squares.

Place on an ungreased cookie sheet. Bake in the preheated oven for 20 to 25 minutes. The shortbread will be mostly white with lightly browned edges.

Makes 16 squares

Notes: To toast pecans, either heat the unchopped nuts in a nonstick skillet, stirring constantly, for 2 or 3 minutes, or place the nuts on a cookie sheet and toast in a 350-degree F oven for 5 to 10 minutes. Stir at least once. Watch carefully as they burn easily.

This recipe does not contain eggs or vanilla.

2 cups unsalted butter

1 cup confectioners' sugar

4 cups all-purpose flour

½ teaspoon baking powder

½ teaspoon salt

½ cup toasted chopped pecans (see note)

RASPBERRY PIE

When raspberries were in season in western Pennsylvania, sometimes as early as Memorial Day but almost always by the Fourth of July, this pie sometimes found its way onto the holiday table at Fallingwater.

CRUST: Preheat the oven to 425 degrees F. In a large bowl, cut the shortening into a mixture of the flour, salt, and sugar until the shortening is the size of cornmeal. Sprinkle on the cold water, a little at a time, until the flour is damp. Mix with a fork until the dough leaves the side of the bowl. Gather into a ball, cut in two pieces, one slightly larger because the bottom crust must be slightly larger than the top. Flatten each, wrap in plastic, and chill for 15 minutes while making the filling.

CRUST

⅔ cup vegetable shortening, chilled

2 cups all-purpose flour

1 teaspoon salt

2 teaspoons sugar

6 to 8 tablespoons cold water

FILLING

5 cups raspberries, washed and patted dry

⅔ cup granulated sugar

6 tablespoons all-purpose flour

¾ teaspoon unflavored gelatin

¼ teaspoon cinnamon

2 teaspoons fresh-squeezed lemon juice

FILLING: In a large bowl, gently mix the sugar, flour, gelatin, and cinnamon. Sprinkle with lemon juice. Fold in the raspberries.

Roll out the bottom crust to fit a 10-inch pie plate.

Carefully spoon the filling into the bottom crust. Put on the top crust, and seal the edges. Cut several holes into the top crust to let the steam escape while baking. To prevent over-browning, put a 2-inch strip of foil around the rim of the crust.

Bake for 45 to 50 minutes; remove the foil for the last 15 minutes of baking time.

Serves 8

RED DEVIL'S FOOD CAKE

Edgar Sr. loved this one-bowl chocolate cake. The food coloring gives it the devilish dark hint of red. After lunch, a big slab of the cake would be wrapped in waxed paper and placed on the kitchen table for Edgar Sr.'s midnight snack. He rambled about the house at all hours, the sound of the waterfall punctuated by his footsteps on the stone.

3½ cups cake flour

2 cups granulated sugar

1 cup brown sugar (light or dark)

2 teaspoons soda

1 teaspoon salt

2⅓ cups buttermilk

1 cup vegetable shortening, softened

4 eggs

4 ounces unsweetened chocolate, melted

2 teaspoons vanilla

1 teaspoon red food coloring

Confectioners' sugar or whipped cream, for serving

Preheat the oven to 350 degrees F.

Butter a 13-by-9-by-2-inch pan.

Into the large bowl of a stand mixer, measure all ingredients. Beat slowly at first, then on high speed until well blended.

Spoon the batter into the prepared pan, smoothing the surface.

Bake for 40 to 45 minutes. Cool in the pan.

To serve, sprinkle with confectioners' sugar or serve with a spoonful of whipped cream. The cake may also be frosted with Chocolate Butter Frosting (recipe page 94), or Peanut Butter Frosting (recipe follows).

Serves 16 to 20

PEANUT BUTTER FROSTING

This favorite frosting recipe comes not from Fallingwater, but from the family farm in Michigan where Suzanne Martinson grew up.

In a bowl, cream the peanut butter and butter with an electric hand mixer until fluffy.

Add the confectioners' sugar, vanilla, and 3 tablespoons of the milk. At low speed, blend until well combined. Beat at medium speed until the frosting is light and fluffy. If the frosting is too stiff, add up to 1 tablespoon of milk to make of spreading consistency.

Slather on the cooled cake.

Enough to frost a 13-by-9-inch cake, or a 2-layer round cake

VARIATION: For Chocolate Peanut Butter Frosting, add 3 ounces unsweetened chocolate, melted, when mixing the peanut butter and butter. If frosting is too thick, add a little more milk. If it is too thin, add more confectioners' sugar.

Note: On the farm, before the microwave was added, baking chocolate was removed from its paper wrapper and melted on an oven-proof saucer while the oven was preheated for the cake. Watch it closely, checking after two minutes, as it can burn. Cool the melted chocolate a little before adding to the other ingredients.

1 cup creamy or crunchy peanut butter (super-crunch is best)

½ cup butter, at room temperature

2 cups confectioners' sugar

2 teaspoons vanilla

3 to 4 tablespoons milk

EDGAR J. KAUFMANN JR. AND THE FALLINGWATER LEGACY

The Dinner Recipes

Edgar J. Kaufmann jr. was devoted to the insistent murmur of the Bear Run waterfall and the home his family built there. It had been his idea to bring in Frank Lloyd Wright when the Kaufmanns began to build, and throughout his lifetime, he propelled his beloved Fallingwater to prominence in the world of twentieth-century architecture.

Edgar jr. studied painting in Europe, including Vienna, Florence, and London, and became a noted art collector, historian, and teacher. Though he was once engaged to a distant cousin favored by his mother, she married someone else. The Kaufmanns hoped their son would one day own their Pittsburgh store, and though Edgar jr. spent time working there in departments including home furnishings, he didn't take to the job of merchant. When it became clear he would not take over the store, it was sold in 1946 to the May Company, though it retained the name Kaufmann's, and Edgar Sr. and Liliane stayed on as the public face of the company. Elsie says that Edgar Sr. always referred to May's purchase of Kaufmann's as a "merger." In 2005, the May Company was acquired by Federated Department Stores, Inc., the parent company of Macy's. Though the Kaufmann's clock, a meeting place for generations of Pittsburghers, still keeps time at Fifth and Smithfield, the store was renamed Macy's.

Edgar J. Kaufmann jr. gave Fallingwater to the Western Pennsylvania Conservancy in 1963. Photograph by Kenneth Love, courtesy of Western Pennsylvania Conservancy.

Edgar jr.'s professional calling was to be a curator at the Museum of Modern Art in New York, and he once observed that his museum job came without benefit of either a high school or college diploma. His independent study honed his facility for languages—in addition to English, he spoke Spanish, German, and Italian. He later taught at Columbia University, but promoting Frank Lloyd Wright and Fallingwater eventually became his life's work.

After the death of his parents, Edgar jr., who lived in New York, retained many of his parents' employees. When he asked Elsie if she would continue to cook for him at Fallingwater, she hedged. "If you're worried about working for Grace Stoops, don't think about that," he said. "I won't allow her to come near Fallingwater."

He insisted that the inside of Fallingwater always appear as beautiful as its setting, and adopted his parents' protocol with the staff. If he found empty vases, there was hell to pay. On one occasion, the staff didn't fill the flower box over the steps leading to the stream. Edgar jr. stopped in unexpectedly for lunch and immediately noticed the missing flowers. He sent the caretaker off to buy some. The man hurried off to Connellsville and Uniontown and "who knows where else," Elsie recalls, returning some time later with $250 worth. He put them in place. "That's fine. That's beautiful," Edgar jr. said and left to have his chauffeur drive him to the airport.

He also insisted that the maids and cook not clean their own rooms—that wasn't their job. Nor should a cook do laundry. One weekend, Edgar jr. wanted to wear a particular shirt back to his apartment in Manhattan. He had dozens of shirts, but he wanted his favorite washed and ironed before he set out. Elsie told him she'd be glad to run it through the washer, but he insisted that the house-keeper, Elsie Harbaugh, should do it. "So she drove ten miles to wash one shirt," Elsie Henderson says.

Edgar jr. knew that managing a staff could involve conflict. When his parents were still alive, an officious housekeeper from their Pittsburgh penthouse had arrived at Fallingwater, unauthorized and unannounced, with her chauffeur boyfriend—to "inventory" the place, according to Elsie. The woman started questioning every item in the kitchen. This infuriated Elsie, they got into a tussle, and she sent the housekeeper back to the city with a black eye. Elsie's co-workers told her she'd be fired for sure. That weekend, Edgar jr., who was visiting from New York, asked his mother where Elsie was. Liliane just smiled and said, "She's taking a week off to cool down."

"She better be cooled off by next weekend, because I've invited friends," he said.

Edgar jr.'s appreciation for Elsie's culinary skills did not diminish later in his life. Sometimes he would fly her to New York for several days to prepare food for his Manhattan parties. "He would always meet me at the airport himself," she remembers. Knowing well her fear of flying, he used to joke, "I'll be there waiting with an ambulance."

Like his parents, Edgar jr. respected his employees, many of whom were black. Elsie remembers his anger when someone typed a staff list with a white employee's name rather than Elsie's at the top.

Edgar Sr. had worked hard at being a gentleman farmer. His son worked just as hard to turn Bear Run Farm into a paying proposition, though it never came close. Although his father liked his farm employees to join him for a bite to eat Monday mornings while they talked over the new week's work, Edgar jr. stopped the practice to save money. The son's businesslike approach extended to Fallingwater's kitchen, Elsie recalls. He even sent her a formal letter to that effect. He asked his employees to keep track of what they spent, and Elsie says she was the only one who came in under budget—about $150 for the season, to her recollection. "Elsie, you're the only one who cares about the budget, so here's a gift for you," Edgar jr. said, handing her a bonus check for that amount. When he wouldn't take it back, she donated it to the Termon Home for Colored Children on Pittsburgh's North Side.

On Fallingwater weekends, Edgar jr. would often meet his longtime companion Paul Mayen at New York's Penn Station after work and catch the train to Greensburg, Pennsylvania, where the chauffeur picked them up for the forty-minute drive to the house. Mayen contributed photographs for an article Edgar jr. wrote for Bruno Zevi's *Architettura VIII* magazine on Fallingwater's twenty-fifth anniversary—one of Edgar jr.'s many efforts to cement the brilliance of Wright's masterpiece internationally.

After the house went to the Western Pennsylvania Conservancy, Edgar jr. asked Mayen, an architect and industrial designer, to create the Visitor Center that today welcomes guests to Fallingwater. Built in 1979, and surrounded by trees and rhododendrons, it includes a gift and bookshop, a café with historic photographs of Fallingwater's construction, and childcare facilities.

Of course, owning a house by a waterfall had its challenges. Fallingwater flooded twice, first in 1954—the stairs to the stream were strengthened after that. Then on a stormy August weekend in 1956, a tornado with heavy rains brought a flash flood down Bear Run. Elsie had just served lunch to Edgar jr. Water swept through the main floor and flooded the basement, destroying the preserves that had just been put up, though the liquor was saved. Two important sculptures were washed away, one never recovered.

As the water rose, Edgar cried, "Elsie! I've got the ham!"

"At lunch you were complaining it was too salty," she said.

"That was then, this is now!" he said. She grabbed the ham from him and carried it up to the guesthouse. There was little damage to the house but it took two months to clean the mud and debris off the floors. Edgar jr. took no chances and called Wright to Bear Run to check on the house's structural stability.

Elsie was instructed to have six employees waiting for Wright on the bridge that crosses the stream where the house sits. One of them was Earl Friend, who'd been on the crew that built Fallingwater. It was his only contact with the architect. "That Buddha belongs outside on the terrace," Wright told him. So Earl, a diminutive 5 foot 2, and Harold Jones, a husky man who towered more than 6 feet tall, each grabbed one side of the heavy sculpture and carried it outside to its prescribed place.

■

In 1963, Edgar jr. gave Fallingwater to the Western Pennsylvania Conservancy to preserve, protect, and share with the public. He wanted the house to feel like a home, not a museum, however, and had a clear idea of how Fallingwater should be presented. Rooms would be open, rather than blocked by velvet cords, like many historic houses. Guests could wander on the terrace and imagine dining there or at the black walnut table near the fireplace. They would be able to browse the titles of Edgar's well-chosen books, and inspect the bed in the master bedroom, with its turned-down sheets of undyed linen. When Fallingwater's rugs or furnishings became worn, they would be replaced. That was Edgar jr.'s vision, and he had spent a lifetime preparing for it.

As a young man, Edgar jr. briefly apprenticed with Wright and knew that design was paramount to the architect. He also knew that his family's tree-trunk tables irritated Wright, but the family kept them as a reminder of the chestnut trees that died in a widespread blight.

He continued to visit the house, though he never stayed there after the Conservancy took ownership. Elsie says she was "in and out" of the house for a year or two greeting and cooking for guests. The Conservancy invited Roger Tory Peterson, the naturalist and artist, to stay at Fallingwater as its first artist-in-residence while he worked on *Birds of the World*.

No longer the master of Fallingwater, Edgar jr. "settled up with the staff," Elsie says, with severance payments commensurate with their length of service. They had no retirement fund.

The house remained true to Wright and the Kaufmann family. The art, sculpture, and fine crafts accumulated over a lifetime decorate the walls, rooms, and terraces. Edgar's, Liliane's, and Edgar jr.'s taste in furnishings are evident in every room. Their books line the stairway. Most important, Fallingwater still connects with the quiet beauty and serenity of Bear Run. Edgar jr. "wanted people to be able to feel what it was like to live there with nature," says Lynda Waggoner, director of Fallingwater. Lynda, who started working at Fallingwater as a guide in high school, says it probably wasn't her education in art and architecture history that convinced Edgar she was a good fit for Fallingwater. He liked the way she arranged flowers, the way his mother liked them. "Liliane liked simple arrangements with only one type of flower," Lynda explains.

As Fallingwater director and vice president of the Conservancy, Lynda observed first-hand Edgar jr.'s "connoisseur's eye" in everything he owned, including his large Park Avenue apartment in New York and his island villa on Hydra in Greece. "At Fallingwater there was not anything that was not thoughtfully chosen," she says.

Edgar jr. had a superb color memory, a rare gift, Lynda says. When the Conservancy wanted to replicate the house's original color, he picked out the paint he remembered as a young man. When the original paint was chemically analyzed, she says, his memory was "right on."

She recalls that Edgar jr. could be "pretty prickly," though they always got along well. He had a gentle way of letting his opinion be known. "When we spoke of doing something he didn't like, he would say, 'You might want to re-think that.'

"We shared a passion for Fallingwater and, of course, I deferred to him."

Edgar jr. would often meet with Tom Schmidt, the first director and former president of the Conservancy, and Lynda at Fallingwater, or they would travel to New York to meet him. She says one trip evolved into "one of the great comedies of all time." They had agreed to be at his Park Avenue apartment after lunch at 1:00 or 1:30 p.m., but arrived in the city early. "Tom and I decided to have lunch at a deli. We had huge corned beef sandwiches and probably fries, too. We were stuffed."

When they arrived at Edgar jr.'s, he had made lunch reservations at a fine restaurant nearby. "It was a five-course lunch," she recalls. "We were good sports—but we didn't eat a lot. I felt absolutely green. I never told him, he was so happy to take us out."

Edgar J. Kaufmann jr. died in 1989. Elsie was asked to receive 125 invited guests at the memorial service in his beloved Fallingwater. As Elsie recalls, she was "about the only black face" there. (Pittsburgh labor organizer Nate Smith also attended.)

Although there was room for him in the crypt designed for his parents, Paul decided to scatter his ashes on the Fallingwater grounds.

In addition to the Greek villa, Paul inherited Edgar jr.'s Manhattan apartment, his country home in New York, and any piece of Edgar jr.'s art collection that had "sentimental value." He professed sentiment for it all and sold the collection at auction for nearly $10 million.

That wasn't the only thing he inherited. Paul Mayen, who died in 2000, told Elsie that Edgar jr. had left him a list of people he was to look out for. "He told me my name was at the top," she says.

A letter that Edgar jr. had written to Elsie illustrates his lasting concern. Long after retiring, she wrote him that she lacked money to pay a doctor's bill. He sent her a check for $146 made out to Robert Cassells, M.D. The envelope also included a $1,200 check made out to Elsie on which was typed the word "gift." Enclosed was a typewritten note:

Dear Elsie,

Please let me know when the enclosed funds begin to get thin? I'm really glad to be of use to you, and will take it as a kindness on your part if you don't hesitate to let me know how to do that. All the best!

The handwritten signature said simply *Edgar.*

Elsie's voice always warms when she talks about Edgar jr., whether discussing his generosity or his foibles. He could be meticulous to a fault. Because of the distance from Pittsburgh, each appliance in Elsie's Fallingwater kitchen had a spare, and often the spare had a spare. "We had to have three mixers, in case one went kerplunk," she remembers.

A few weeks before Fallingwater was turned over to the Conservancy, one Mixmaster broke. Edgar insisted on buying another. Elsie argued that it seemed like an unnecessary expense because they already had two others that still worked fine, but he was adamant. When they closed the house, she inherited the new Mixmaster.

It still works.

Braided Challah. Photograph by Linda Mitzel.

THE DINNER RECIPES

When the Kaufmanns entertained people for dinner at Fallingwater, after everyone had eaten there was often dancing to 78 rpm records on the built-in Capehart player. The gregarious Edgar Sr. would call into the kitchen and drag Elsie out to meet his guests. Sometimes he danced with her. His company looked askance. "They must have been thinking, 'He dances with the hired help!'" Elsie says.

MAIN DISHES

GRILLED TROUT

After Fallingwater was built, the Kaufmanns stocked the upper part of Bear Run creek above the house with brown trout. The stream was posted for trespassers, and Edgar Sr. hired people to patrol its banks for interlopers.

Bill Scarlett grew up on the farm of his grandparents, Charles and Rebecca Tissue. He was attending the one-room schoolhouse that sat on the Tissue property and described himself a "just a small snot then."

Bill must have been only six years old or so that summer day he took off to go fishing. "It was posted, but I didn't pay any attention to that. I got a branch and tied a string with a hook on it with some bait, and went fishing in the baptizing hole."

The hole was close to the road, but he was so intent waiting for something to bite that he didn't hear anybody approach.

"Are you catching any, Billy?" a deep voice asked. It was Edgar Sr.

The boy, who was about "scared out of his britches," wondered, "Do I jump in the water and run?"

But Edgar Sr. seemed happy to see him. "Have a good time, and catch some fish," he told the astonished boy.

½ cup unsalted butter

1 tablespoon grated lemon peel

¼ cup fresh lemon juice

2 tablespoons chopped fresh mint

3 garlic cloves, minced

4 12-ounce trout fillets, with skin (brown, brook, or rainbow trout)

Salt and freshly ground black pepper

⅔ cups sliced almonds, toasted

Combine the butter, lemon peel, lemon juice, mint, and garlic in a small saucepan. Whisk over medium-low heat until the butter melts and the mixture is blended.

To prepare the grill, brush the grate with vegetable oil and ignite the briquettes. When the briquettes are covered with gray ash, spread out to cover the bottom of the grill, one briquette deep, for medium heat.

Brush the flesh side of the fillets with some of the lemon butter. Sprinkle with salt and pepper.

Grill the fish, covered, flesh side down, until the fillets begin to brown, about 1½ minutes. Using a large metal spatula, turn the trout over and brush with additional lemon butter. Grill, covered, until cooked through, about 2 minutes longer. The flesh should be flaky but still moist.

Grilled Trout, often made with fresh fish caught in Bear Run, accompanied by Hot and Crispy Cukes. Photograph by Linda Mitzel.

Transfer the trout to heated plates, skin side down. Bring the remaining lemon butter to a boil and drizzle over the trout. Sprinkle the trout with toasted almonds and serve.

Serves 4

Note: Elsie Henderson says that grilled and broiled fish were often served with Hot and Crispy Cukes (please see recipe on page 83). When serving fresh fish, allow ½ pound per person.

SCALLOPED OYSTERS

Fresh oysters were not inexpensive, but the Kaufmanns didn't fret about that. In their day, oysters were best in the months ending with an r, though today many oysters are farm-raised and under tighter federal seafood regulations.

1 quart large oysters, including juice

1 cup whipping cream

5 cups soft bread crumbs

¾ cup butter, melted

1½ teaspoons celery seed

Dash of salt

½ teaspoon black pepper

Preheat oven to 375 degrees F.

Butter a 10-by-13-inch baking dish.

Arrange the oysters, including the juice, in the baking dish.

Pour over the cream. Combine the bread crumbs, butter, celery seed, salt, and pepper. Spoon over the oysters.

Bake, uncovered, about 45 minutes. The top will be brown.

Serves 8

LIVER AND ONIONS

Edgar Kaufmann Sr. was fond of calves' liver, which he enjoyed served with bacon and caramelized onions. Given a high-quality calf's liver, this recipe could inspire a conversion to liver and onions.

1 calf's liver (¾ to 1 pound)

3 tablespoons butter

Flour seasoned with salt and pepper to taste

Butter

½ pound lean bacon

1 large white onion, peeled, sliced, and separated into rings

Ask the butcher to cut the liver ½-inch thick. Remove all the membrane.

Dip the liver into seasoned flour. Shake off any excess flour. In a frying pan, brown the floured liver in butter on medium-high heat, about 3 minutes on each side. Remove and keep warm.

Brown the onion in the butter, adding additional butter to the pan as needed. Sauté until soft. Remove the caramelized, browned onion; keep warm. Serve with the liver.

In the same frying pan, fry the bacon until very crisp. Drain on paper towels. Serve with the liver and onions.

Serves 3 or 4

LOBSTER BISQUE

In Elsie Henderson's cooking repertoire, this recipe is a rarity, because it contains the ubiquitous condensed cream of tomato soup. Canned soup has been used in recipes for many years, but its popularity reached its zenith in the 1950s and 1960s following the 1941 publication of Campbell Soup Company's Easy Ways to Good Meals *cookbook. Subsequent cookbooks popularized it as an ingredient in everything from main dishes to vegetables, even desserts. The flavor of this delicious bisque has just a hint of a taste of the green peas as a complement to the lobster.*

Shell enough fresh peas to make 2 cups. In a small saucepan, cover the peas with water, add the salt, and cook until soft; drain. Put the peas through a blender with the soup; blend until smooth.

In a large separate pan, heat the milk and cream. Do NOT allow to boil. Add the black pepper and Worcestershire. Stir in the lobster and sherry.

Combine the two liquids, reheat, and serve.

Serves 6 to 8

Fresh green peas, about 2 to 3 pints

1 can condensed cream of tomato soup, undiluted

1 teaspoon salt

2 cups whole milk

1 cup whipping cream

½ teaspoon freshly ground black pepper

1 teaspoon Worcestershire sauce

2 pounds lobster meat, cut into bite-sized pieces

⅓ cup very dry sherry (not cooking sherry)

BAKED SHRIMP AND CRAB CASSEROLE

This casserole is easy to make and gives the home cook time to circulate among the guests. In the informal atmosphere of Fallingwater, Elsie Henderson's recipes for the family ranged from her simple creamed chicken in toast cups to European sweetbreads. Mourning doves—served three to a plate and presented with lemon sauce—were served when there were guests.

Preheat the oven to 350 degrees F.

Chop the green pepper, onion, and celery into fine pieces and mix in a bowl.

Add the crab and shrimp. Stir in the Boiled Salad Dressing, sour cream, Worcestershire sauce, Old Bay, salt, and white pepper.

Toss the bread crumbs with the melted butter.

1 small green pepper

1 small onion

1 cup celery

1 pound back fin crab, rinsed well

1 pound medium shrimp, cleaned and deveined

⅓ cup Boiled Salad Dressing (recipe page 53)

(Ingredients are continued)

⅓ cup sour cream

1 teaspoon Worcestershire sauce

1 teaspoon Old Bay seasoning

1 teaspoon salt

⅛ teaspoon white pepper

1½ cup dry bread crumbs

¼ cup melted butter

Standing rib beef roast (5 pounds or more)

YORKSHIRE PUDDING

4 large eggs

2 cups milk, whole or low-fat

2 cups sifted all-purpose flour

1 teaspoon salt

1 tablespoon butter

Place the seafood mixture into a 2-quart buttered casserole. Sprinkle with the buttered crumbs.

Bake, uncovered, for 35 to 40 minutes. It will bubble, and the top will be browned.

Serves 4 to 6

ROAST BEEF WITH YORKSHIRE PUDDING

ROAST: Preheat the oven to 550 degrees F. Place the meat, fat side up, on the rack of a roaster pan. Immediately reduce the heat to 350 degrees F. Roast approximately 18 to 20 minutes per pound for medium rare.

When the roast reaches an internal temperature of 145 degrees F, remove it from oven and let stand before carving.

YORKSHIRE PUDDING: Set the oven to 425 degrees F. In a bowl, blend the eggs, milk, flour, and salt with either a hand mixer or a whisk. About ½ hour before the beef is done, spoon about ½ cup of the drippings from the beef into a 9-by-13-inch pan and add the butter. The butter should melt in the hot drippings. Carefully pour in the batter.

Bake 25 minutes, then lower heat to 350 degrees F and bake an additional 9 to 15 minutes. When done, the Yorkshire Pudding should be nicely browned.

Cut into squares and serve around the platter of beef.

1 pound of beef serves 3 to 4 people

Yorkshire Pudding serves 15 to 20 as an accompaniment

ROASTED BELGIAN HARE

In Elsie Henderson's time at Fallingwater, one of the leading butchers in Pittsburgh was a man she knew only as Carver, who did business in Pittsburgh's Market Square. The Kaufmanns dealt with him almost exclusively, and he furnished the hare that the family loved so much.

Have the butcher quarter the hare.

Season the hare lightly with salt, pepper, and marjoram.

In a large pan with a wire rack, roast the hare, skin side up, in a 375-degree F oven for about 20 minutes. Turn and finish roasting it for about 35 minutes. The skin will be brown and crispy, and the internal temperature should be 150 degrees F.

Serves 4 to 6

Note: Belgian hare is a breed of domesticated rabbit, which came from Flanders to England in 1874 and arrived in America fourteen years later. The hares' popularity tapered off, and they are rare today, when much of the commercially sold rabbit meat comes frozen from China.

1 Belgian hare (about 4 pounds), or other breed

Salt and freshly ground pepper

Marjoram to taste

HAM LOAF

This delicious recipe makes two loaves, so one can be served immediately, and the second frozen to be baked later (see note). Edgar Sr. loved this ham loaf and it wasn't unusual to see him walking around Fallingwater munching on a slice.

Preheat the oven to 350 degrees F.

In a large bowl, mix the ground meats with the eggs, milk, and pepper. Stir in the bread crumbs. (Mixing works best when done with the hands.) Lightly pack the meat mixture into two 9-by-5-by-2½-inch loaf pans.

In a small bowl, mix the mustard and brown sugar together. Divide equally, spreading half of the mixture over each loaf.

Bake in the preheated oven for 1½ hours.

HAM LOAF

2 pounds ground ham

1 pound ground veal

1 pound ground pork

4 eggs, beaten

1½ cups milk

Coarsely ground black pepper to taste

1½ cups whole wheat bread crumbs

(Ingredients are continued)

TOPPING

½ tablespoon prepared mustard

½ cup brown sugar, packed

Drain the fat and let the loaves set for a few minutes before slicing for serving.

Each loaf serves 6 to 8

Note: To freeze the second loaf for later, line the loaf pan with heavy-duty aluminum foil, add half the meat mixture, and place it in the freezer. When the meat is frozen, remove the loaf from the pan and double-wrap securely. If cooking without thawing first, add 15 to 20 minutes to the baking time.

Ham Loaf, one of Edgar Sr.'s favorites.
Photograph by Linda Mitzel.

SALADS AND SIDE DISHES

HOT AND CRISPY CUKES

Elsie Henderson liked to serve this hot vegetable any time the Kaufmanns were having fish for dinner.

Pare the cucumbers, halve lengthwise, and remove the seeds (a grapefruit spoon works well). Cut into large cubes or slices.

In a large saucepan, cook the cucumbers in Chicken Broth and butter.

Do not overcook. The cukes should be crisp.

Serve hot with fish.

Serves 8 as a side dish

6 to 9 cucumbers

1 cup Chicken Broth (recipe page 49)

2 tablespoons butter

FRESH SALAD

This salad is as beautiful as it is simple. All three Kaufmanns were friends of artist Frida Kahlo and her husband, muralist and painter Diego Rivera, whom they visited in Mexico, where avocados, once called alligator pears, originated. Although the artists' visits were before Elsie's tenure at Fallingwater, she prepared some dishes influenced by Mexican cuisine.

Peel the avocado and cut it into ¼-inch slices, discarding the pit. Sprinkle with lemon juice and a pinch of salt.

Section the peeled oranges and grapefruits. If large, sections may be cut in half.

Arrange the citrus fruit and avocado slices, and garnish with watercress.

Dust with the confectioners' sugar.

Serves 6 to 8

2 ripe avocados

Fresh-squeezed lemon juice

Salt

2 large navel oranges, peeled

2 grapefruits, peeled

Watercress for garnish

2 tablespoons confectioners' sugar

WALDORF SALAD

This is a good salad, because apples have long been wintered over, and so the ingredients are available year-round. The toasted pecans are a variation on the more familiar walnuts found in many recipes.

½ cup Boiled Salad Dressing (recipe page 53)

4 cups cored, peeled, and diced apple

2 cups finely chopped celery

⅔ cup coarsely chopped toasted pecans

Hearts of Bibb lettuce

Prepare salad dressing and allow to cool.

Combine the remaining ingredients, add dressing, and toss lightly.

Serve on hearts of Bibb lettuce on individual plates.

To toast pecans: Put the nuts in a hot, ungreased sauté pan for 3 or 4 minutes, stirring constantly, or place the nuts on a cookie sheet for 7 to 10 minutes in a 350-degree F oven.

Serves 4 to 6

Note: For more color, unblemished apples may be left unpeeled. A combination of yellow and red apples is another fine variation.

DEEP-FRIED ONION RINGS

Onion Rings were a favorite accompaniment to steak cooked outside on the charcoal grill. Given the workout that guests got hiking and swimming, their appetites were hearty.

2 large Spanish onions

1 cup all-purpose flour

½ teaspoon salt

1 teaspoon baking powder

1⅓ cups whole milk, approximately

Vegetable oil

Remove the outer layer from the onions. Slice the onions about ¼ inch thick. Separate into rings. Cover the sliced onions with cold water and let stand 30 minutes in a bowl, while the batter is being made.

Mix the flour, salt, baking powder, and milk in a small bowl. Drain the onions on paper towels.

Into a sauté or frying pan, pour enough oil so that it is about 1 inch deep. Heat the oil to 375 degrees F. When the oil is hot enough, a drop of water will skip and sizzle in the oil.

Dip the onion rings, one at a time, in the batter. Allow the excess batter to drip into the bowl.

Fry a few onion rings at a time, turning once with tongs.

Drain well on paper towels.

Keep in a warm oven until ready to serve.

Serves 4 or 5

LILIANE'S GUACAMOLE

Fallingwater guests mixed themselves a drink from the extensive array of liquors that the Kaufmanns kept on a brass tray on the chestnut log table in front of the fireplace. Socializing before dinner, they dipped into this Mexican appetizer. Liliane Kaufmann, who enjoyed Mexican food, loved to drink exotic mixed drinks. Busy in the kitchen, Elsie never exactly knew what went into their libations.

Working carefully, cut at least one avocado (or more, depending on the number of guests) in half lengthwise and retain its shell. Remove the pit and scoop out the flesh of the fruit.

For the rest of the avocados, peel, pit, and mash the avocados (6 if small, 2 if large). Discard any discolored spots in the fruits. Finely chop the tomatoes and jalapeno (also seeded, with interior ribs removed) and mix with the salt, pepper, and lemon juice. Add the fresh cilantro and garlic to taste. Mix well.

Present the guacamole in the avocado shell(s).

Serve immediately with toast fingers. Guacamole is also good as a dip with tortillas or as a topping for chili.

Serves about 10 as a dip

Note: To easily remove the skin from the tomatoes, drop in boiling water for a few seconds. The skin will come right off.

4 ripe avocados

2 small onions, finely chopped

2 peeled and seeded tomatoes

4 chili peppers (jalapeno or other)

2 teaspoons salt

1 teaspoon coarsely ground pepper

2 tablespoons freshly squeezed lemon juice

Chopped cilantro and minced garlic to taste

HOLLANDAISE SAUCE

In warm weather, the butler cooked outdoors on the grill. Elsie Henderson made all the sauces. Hollandaise was the favorite sauce for vegetables, and Béarnaise was a satisfying sauce for steaks. Unlike the Hollandaise made for Eggs Benedict, which contains Tabasco, this one does not.

3 egg yolks (see note)

1 tablespoon freshly squeezed lemon juice

½ teaspoon salt

½ cup melted butter

In a blender, mix the egg yolks, lemon juice, and salt on low speed; as it blends, slowly pour in the melted butter and mix.

Makes about 1 cup

Notes: This sauce is excellent served over asparagus that has been steamed or roasted.

Because of the danger of Salmonella enteritidis in uncooked egg yolks, pasteurized eggs are recommended, especially if the diners are very young, very old, or suffering from a weakened immune system.

BÉARNAISE SAUCE

This sauce was a Fallingwater staple whenever grilled T-bone or Porterhouse beef steaks were served. It can be served atop the grilled steaks or on the side.

1 cup Hollandaise Sauce (recipe above)

½ teaspoon minced onion

½ teaspoon tarragon leaves

¼ teaspoon chervil leaves

1 tablespoon white vinegar

To the prepared Hollandaise Sauce, add the onion, herbs, and vinegar. Mix well.

Makes about 1 cup

ROQUEFORT COLESLAW

The Roquefort, or blue, cheese adds the gourmet touch to this salad, an excellent accompaniment to fish or fowl.

In a large bowl, toss the cabbage and chopped onion.

Blend the sour cream, salad dressing, salt, dry mustard, and pepper. Add the blue cheese.

Pour over the cabbage and toss well. Serve immediately for a crisp salad, or refrigerate overnight for a marinated flavor and texture.

Serves 4 to 6

Note: A combination of red and green cabbage adds color to this salad.

4 cups finely chopped cabbage

⅓ cup chopped onion

½ cup sour cream

¼ cup Boiled Salad Dressing (recipe page 53)

½ teaspoon salt

½ teaspoon dry mustard

Freshly ground pepper to taste

¼ cup Roquefort, or blue, cheese

SPOON BREAD

Although this satisfying dish is referred to as "bread," it more closely resembles a vegetable side dish. It is popular in the South, where Elsie's grandparents ran a small store in Front Royal, Virginia. She often spent summers there, and she enjoyed watching her grandmother, who was Cherokee, ride sidesaddle on her horse. Sometimes her grandmother, wise in the ways of the rural South, scolded Elsie for being too "uppity" around the white folks. "You're not in Pittsburgh now," she told the little girl.

Preheat oven to 375 degrees F.

Add the boiling water to the cornmeal, stirring constantly to prevent lumps. Let cool.

Stir in the melted butter, egg yolks, buttermilk, salt, sugar, baking powder, and baking soda.

In a separate bowl, beat the egg whites until soft peaks form, and carefully fold into the batter.

Pour into a 2-quart greased casserole and bake for 45 to 50 minutes.

Serve hot with additional butter.

Serves 8 as a side dish

1½ cups boiling water

1 cup cornmeal

¼ cup melted butter

3 eggs, separated

1 cup buttermilk

1 teaspoon salt

1 teaspoon sugar

1 teaspoon baking powder

¼ teaspoon soda

Additional butter

BREAD AND ROLLS

RICH BREAD

This versatile bread dough can be used not only for everyday bread, but for sweet and savory variations. The directions for Cinnamon Rolls and Caraway Twists follow this basic recipe, and the following recipe, for Raisin Bread, also uses Elsie's Rich Bread dough.

2 packages dry yeast, or 2 scant tablespoons bulk yeast

½ cup warm water (110 degrees F)

1½ cups milk, scalded and cooled to lukewarm

¼ cup granulated sugar

1 teaspoon salt

3 large eggs, at room temperature

¼ cup butter, melted and cooled to lukewarm

About 7½ cups all-purpose flour

In a large bowl or in the bowl of an electric stand mixer, dissolve the yeast in warm water. Add the warm milk, sugar, salt, eggs, and butter. Mix well to combine.

Mix in the flour, starting with 6 cups. To the batter, add additional flour, a little at a time, until the dough is easy to handle (if making by hand) or comes away from the side of the bowl (if using a mixer). On a lightly floured board, knead the dough until smooth.

Form the dough into a ball. Place in a well-greased bowl, turning the dough over so that the shortening coats all surfaces. Cover the dough with a towel and let it rise in a warm place until double, about 1 to 1½ hours.

Divide the dough and place it in two well-greased 9-by-5-by-3-inch bread pans. Cover and let rise until double, about 1 hour.

Bake in a preheated 425-degree F oven for 30 to 35 minutes. Remove from the pans immediately. For a soft crust, lightly brush the bread with butter. Cool slightly before cutting with a serrated bread knife.

Makes 2 loaves

Note: You can also shape the dough for bread by rolling the dough out on a lightly floured surface into a rectangle the width of the 9-inch loaf pan (the dough will be about twice that long). Then roll up the rectangle, starting at the 9-inch side, pressing with each turn. Pinch the end of the dough and the ends to seal. The roll should be baked seam-side-down.

CINNAMON ROLLS: Follow recipe for Rich Bread. Using half of the dough, roll into a rectangle, about ½-inch thick. Brush ¼ cup soft butter on the dough, then sprinkle with a mixture of ½ cup light brown sugar and ½ teaspoon cinnamon. Starting on the long side, roll up, pinching the end into the roll. Cut the roll into

1½- to 2-inch slices; place in buttered cupcake pan. Brush with melted butter. Let rise until double. Bake in 350-degree F oven for 15 to 25 minutes, or until light brown. Cool rolls on wire rack. The cooled rolls may be drizzled with confectioners' sugar mixed with a little cream and ¼ teaspoon vanilla.

Makes about 1 dozen

CARAWAY TWISTS: Follow recipe for Rich Bread. Using half of the dough, roll into a rectangle ½ inch thick and about 8 by 16 inches. Cut dough into 1-by-8-inch strips. Take two strips, pinch ends together, and twist. Brush with melted butter and roll in caraway seeds, about 2 tablespoons for all. Place on greased cookie sheet, cover, and let rise until double. Bake in 350-degree F oven for 6 to 10 minutes, until lightly brown. Serve warm, or cool on wire rack.

Makes 8 twists

RAISIN BREAD

Roll the dough out into large circle. Spread with the soft butter and sprinkle with the brown sugar, which has been mixed with cinnamon and nutmeg. Sprinkle on the raisins.

Roll up tightly. Seal the end. Place the roll in a well-greased Bundt pan or angel food cake pan.

Cover with a towel or plastic wrap misted with vegetable spray. Let rise until double.

Bake in a preheated 375-degree F oven for 40 to 45 minutes.

Remove immediately from pan. Cool on wire rack.

Makes 1 loaf in Bundt or angel food pan

Note: The time it takes for dough to rise varies dramatically, depending on the activity of the yeast, the humidity, and the warmth of the kitchen. It's easier to keep track of rising dough when it's covered with a sheet of see-through plastic wrap that has been sprayed with vegetable oil.

½ of Rich Bread recipe (recipe page 88)

¼ cup soft butter

½ cup light brown sugar

¼ teaspoon cinnamon

Pinch of nutmeg

1 cup golden or dark raisins

CHALLAH

Elsie Henderson arose early to make this bread so beloved by so many of the Kaufmanns' guests. This beautiful bread is great for sandwiches and spectacular in French toast.

1 package dry yeast

¾ cup warm water

½ cup granulated sugar

½ teaspoon salt

3 eggs plus 1 yolk (reserve white)

½ cup butter, softened

2 cups all-purpose flour to start, more as needed (about an additional 2½ to 2¾ cups

1 tablespoon sugar

In a large bowl, dissolve the yeast in the warm water with a sprinkling of the sugar. Let set for 10 minutes to proof the yeast (see note).

Add the remainder of the ½ cup sugar, salt, eggs, egg yolk, and butter. Add the 2 cups flour and blend well with a wooden spoon. The mixture will resemble cake batter. Add enough flour, a little at a time, to make a soft dough. Knead the dough lightly on a floured board. The dough should be neither sticky nor dry to the touch.

Alternately, make dough in a stand electric mixer. Inserting the beater, mix the sugar and butter until smooth. Add the yeast, eggs, yolk, and salt; mix well. Add 2 cups flour and mix well. Replace the regular beater with the dough hook, and add more flour gradually, scraping the bowl often, until the dough comes away from the side of the bowl and forms a ball, using about 2½ cups additional flour. The dough should be neither sticky nor dry to the touch.

Knead on a floured board, about 5 to 8 minutes. Put the dough in a large buttered bowl, cover, and let it rise in a warm place, 1 to 2 hours, until doubled in size.

Punch down the dough, and knead it until it is elastic. Divide the dough into thirds, roll between the palms of the hands into long, round strips and braid; tuck in the loose ends. Place the braid on a greased cookie sheet or use parchment paper. Cover the braid and let it rise in a warm place, or until double, about 1½ to 2 hours.

Preheat the oven to 375 degrees F.

Beat the remaining egg white with the 1 tablespoon sugar. Brush over the bread dough.

Bake for 35 to 45 minutes. The bread will be golden brown and sound hollow when thumped with a thumb.

Remove from the pan.

Makes 1 braided loaf

Note: Most modern-day yeast does not require proofing, as long as the expiration date on the package hasn't run out. To proof yeast, add it to warm water with a little sugar to feed the yeast. It should create bubbles. Yeast, a living plant, should be stored in a cool place or, especially when bought in bulk, in the refrigerator.

ELSIE'S MOTHER'S POTATO BREAD

When Elsie Henderson was a little girl, her mother would call her to the kitchen of their apartment on Pittsburgh's Mount Washington, and say, "Elsie, put on a potato to boil." And Elsie would know that it was time for her mother to bake bread for the family, which included one older sister and eleven strapping brothers. "Imagine my surprise when, as an adult, I began to see potato bread sold in the grocery store as some sort of fancy food," Elsie, who is in her nineties, says. Her potato-bread baking was limited to her own home, however, as the Kaufmanns generally spurned potatoes.

Peel and chop the potato. In a small saucepan, cover the potato with water and bring to a boil. Simmer until the potato is done; it will break when pressed with a fork. Drain the potato water, reserving 1 cup. Set aside the cooked mashed potato, if using.

In the large bowl of an electric mixer, combine the warm potato water and milk.

Add the shortening (lard or vegetable shortening) to the warm liquids and let it melt. Mix in the sugar, salt, and yeast. Add the eggs, which have been lightly beaten with a fork, and mix well.

Add 4 to 5 cups of flour, and the mashed potato, if using. Gradually add the remaining flour, as needed, until a soft dough is formed.

To make the dough easy to handle, turn onto a lightly floured board and knead it until smooth, adding flour as needed to avoid sticking. The dough will begin to develop blisters on the surface when it is kneaded enough.

Place the dough in a large buttered bowl; cover, and let it rise in a warm place until doubled in size, about 1 hour. The dough is ready when it holds its shape when indented with a forefinger.

Punch the dough down and knead again. Divide the dough into thirds. Shape

1 cup lukewarm potato water

Optional: 1 potato, mashed (about 1 cup)

1 cup lukewarm milk

¼ cup sugar

1 tablespoon salt

¼ cup lard (today Elsie uses vegetable shortening)

1 tablespoon dry yeast, dissolved in warm water with a sprinkle of sugar

3 eggs, at room temperature

7 to 7½ cups all-purpose flour

Butter

into three loaves. Put the dough into buttered bread pans and let it rise again until the dough reaches the top of the pans.

Bake in a preheated 425-degree F oven for 35 to 40 minutes, until brown. The bread will sound hollow when tapped.

Turn out of the pan immediately and set on a cooling rack. Brush with melted butter.

Makes 3 loaves

Note: Other options for the dough include Potato Rolls and Potato Hamburger Buns—see the following recipes.

PULL-APART POTATO ROLLS

⅓ of Elsie's Mother's Potato Bread dough (recipe page 91)
Butter, softened

Divide the dough into 36 balls (each will be about 1 inch).

Grease 12 muffin cups with vegetable shortening or coat with nonstick vegetable spray. Drop 3 balls in each cup. Brush with butter.

Cover and let rise 1 hour, or until the dough doubles in size and fills the cups.

Preheat the oven to 400 degrees F. Bake for 13 to 15 minutes, or until brown.

Makes 12 rolls

POTATO BREAD HAMBURGER BUNS

⅓ of Elsie's Mother's Potato Bread dough (recipe page 91)
Sesame seeds or poppy seeds, optional
Butter, softened

Grease a cookie sheet with shortening or nonstick spray. Alternately, use parchment paper.

Working on a lightly floured surface, divide the dough into 12 equal parts. With greased fingertips, shape each part into a ball. Flatten with the palm of the hand. Place the flattened dough about 1 inch apart on a greased cookie sheet and let rise until double in size.

Preheat the oven to 400 degrees F. Brush the buns with butter and sprinkle with poppy or sesame seeds. Bake 13 to 15 minutes. The buns will be golden brown. Put on a wire rack to cook. With a serrated knife, slice for sandwiches.

Makes 12 hamburger buns

Note: To control the amount of flour on the bread board, place some flour in the sifter and sift out a little flour at a time onto the surface where the dough is being kneaded. To reduce the mess between uses, store the sifter on a saucer in the cupboard.

DESSERTS

MR. K'S CHOCOLATE CAKE

Elsie Henderson jokes about how much "you white people" love chocolate, an obsession she does not share. The texture of this delicious one-bowl cake, which Edgar Kaufmann Sr. loved, is more like a frosted brownie.

Preheat the oven to 350 degrees F.

Butter and flour a 9-by-13-by-2-inch pan, or two 9-inch round cake pans.

Measure all the ingredients. Into the large mixing bowl of a stand mixer, starting with the shortening, sugar, and eggs, combine the ingredients, beating well. Add all the other ingredients, and mix at low speed, scraping the bowl often with a rubber spatula.

When well blended, beat at medium high speed for 3 to 4 minutes. Pour into the well-greased pan. Bake from 40 to 45 minutes. Cool. Spread with Chocolate Butter Frosting.

Mr. K's Chocolate Cake can also be made in a Bundt pan. Bake in a 350-degree F oven for 40 to 50 minutes, or until knife inserted in the middle of the cake comes out clean.

Makes 1 9-by-13-inch loaf cake, serving about 18

Note: Rather than greasing the cake pans, another option is to line the bottom of the pans with waxed paper, which makes it easier to turn out the baked layers.

¾ cup vegetable shortening, softened

1⅔ cups granulated sugar

2 eggs

2¼ cups cake flour

⅔ cup unsweetened cocoa

1 teaspoon salt

1 teaspoon baking powder

1¼ cups water

1 teaspoon vanilla

Chocolate Butter Frosting (recipe follows)

CHOCOLATE BUTTER FROSTING

⅔ cup butter, softened

4 ounces unsweetened chocolate, melted

4 cups confectioners' sugar

3 teaspoons vanilla

About 4 tablespoons whole milk

Mix all the ingredients thoroughly, adding enough milk to achieve spreading consistency. Spread on the cooled cake.

Makes enough frosting for a 9-by-13-inch cake

CREAM PUFFS

This appealing dessert looks difficult to do, but with a little concentration it couldn't be easier. It's impressive, too. Fillings can be as simple as sweetened whipped cream, home-made ice cream, or pudding.

1 cup hot water

½ cup butter, softened

1 cup all-purpose flour

4 eggs, at room temperature

Filling of choice (sweetened whipped cream, ice cream, or pudding)

Confectioners' sugar for dusting

Preheat the oven to 400 degrees F.

In a saucepan, heat the water to boiling. Add the butter and flour. Reduce the heat to low. Stir vigorously until the mixture forms a ball. Remove the pan from the heat and add the eggs, one at a time, beating until smooth after each addition.

Drop the dough by about ¼ cupfuls 3 inches apart on an ungreased baking sheet.

Bake for 30 to 40 minutes until puffed and golden. Do not open the oven until they have puffed. They typically double in size. Remove from the oven and make a small slit or two to let the steam escape.

Cool, cut off the tops and pull out any gummy dough.

Fill with ice cream, pudding, or whipped cream and replace the tops. Dust with confectioners' sugar.

Makes 12 to 24 depending on the size

Notes: This steam-leavened dessert requires no baking powder or soda.

It's a bit like gilding the lily, but instead of confectioners' sugar, melted chocolate can be drizzled over the puffs. The same recipe can be used for savory fillings, such as chicken salad or crab. If serving as an appetizer, make half as large.

Whipped cream for Cream Puffs would have come from the Kaufmanns' Jersey cows. Photograph by Linda Mitzel.

BLUEBERRY LATTICE PIE

Fallingwater is not air conditioned and, though western Pennsylvania can be sticky in the summer, its design provides cross breezes from the many windows, except for the kitchen, which has but one. In any case, the sight of a fresh-baked pie cooling on the windowsill is worth any extra heat the oven puts out.

CRUST

2⅔ cups all-purpose flour

1 teaspoon salt

⅔ cup vegetable shortening

4 tablespoons lard

4 tablespoons cold water

FILLING

5 to 6 cups fresh blueberries

¾ cup granulated sugar

¼ cup plus 2 tablespoons flour

½ teaspoon cinnamon

2 teaspoons lemon juice

Preheat the oven to 425 degrees F.

Measure the salt and flour into a large bowl. Cut in the shortening and lard thoroughly with either a pastry blender or two knives.

Sprinkle in the water, 1 tablespoon at a time, until the flour is moistened and the dough ball cleaves to the side of the bowl.

With your hands, form the dough into a smooth ball, divide, and refrigerate until well chilled, especially if it's a warm summer day. Allow a little more dough for the bottom crust than the top.

For the bottom crust, with a rolling pin, shape the dough into a circle 1 inch larger than the 9- or 10-inch pie pan. Fit it loosely in the pie plate.

For the filling, mix the fresh blueberries with the remaining flour, sugar, cinnamon, and lemon juice. Fill the lower crust.

Roll out the remaining pastry, and cut into 10 to 12 lattice strips. Interweave them to make a lattice top.

Bake the pie for 45 to 50 minutes. Place a piece of foil around the rim if the pie browns too quickly. Do not press down.

Serves 8

Note: If the blueberries are quite juicy, Elsie suggests adding a teaspoon of Knox unflavored gelatin to the filling.

Elsie Henderson shows how to weave a lattice crust for a berry pie. Photograph by Rob Long.

LEMON CHIFFON PIE

This luscious, light pie was one of the Kaufmanns' favorite endings to a company meal. Its airiness comes from the whipped egg whites that are folded into the filling.

Baked 9-inch pie shell (recipe page 103; adapted as explained in recipe directions at right)

½ cup granulated sugar

1 envelope Knox unflavored gelatin

4 egg yolks (reserve the whites)

⅔ cup water

⅓ cup freshly squeezed lemon juice

1 tablespoon grated lemon peel

4 egg whites, at room temperature

⅓ teaspoon cream of tartar

½ cup granulated sugar

Whipped cream for decorating

Use crust recipe from page 103 but omit pecans. Preheat the oven to 450 degrees F. Ease pastry into pie pan, flute, and prick the bottom and sides with a fork. Bake for 8 to 10 minutes, until lightly browned. Cool before filling.

Stir together the ½ cup sugar and gelatin. Mix the egg yolks, water, and lemon juice into the sugar mixture.

In a saucepan, cook the mixture over medium heat, stirring constantly, until it comes to a boil. Remove from the heat and stir in the grated lemon peel.

Chill in the refrigerator, stirring occasionally, until the mixture mounds when dropped from a spoon.

To complete the filling, in a large bowl of the electric mixer, beat the egg whites with the cream of tartar until foamy. Beat in the remaining ½ cup sugar, 1 tablespoon at a time, until the mixture is thick and glossy. Fold the lemon mixture into the whipped egg whites. Pile into the prebaked pie shell.

Chill two or three hours.

Decorate with sweetened whipped cream. Refrigerate any leftover pie.

Serves 6

Notes: "Light" cream will not whip, nor will half and half. A good topping is made with heavy cream, which typically doubles in volume when whipped. Extra-heavy whipping cream may also be used, but watch it closely because it can quickly turn into butter as it's whipped. Some cooks like to sweeten whipped cream with a little confectioners' or granulated sugar and add vanilla or other extracts, such as almond.

Here's a tip for the beginning cook. Wash the lemon and grate its peel *before* extracting the lemon juice. A Microplane or other brand of long grater will give a zest, or peel, without any of the bitter white.

CLOVE CAKE

This cake was one of Edgar Sr.'s favorites, and he often enjoyed it with a glass of milk from the farm's cows.

Preheat the oven to 350 degrees F. Butter a 10-inch tube or Bundt pan.

In the large bowl of an electric mixer, cream the butter and sugar until smooth and fluffy.

In a small bowl, beat the eggs until they are lemon-colored. Beat them into the butter-sugar mixture.

Into another large bowl, sift the flour, cinnamon, cloves, and salt.

In a second small bowl, combine the milk and lemon juice; let the mixture stand undisturbed for 5 minutes, or until it is thickened.

Add to the butter-sugar-egg mixture in the electric mixer bowl one-third of the flour mixture and one-half of the milk mixture, combining well.

Add another one-third of the flour mixture. Add the baking soda to the remaining milk mixture. Combine that with the batter in the electric mixer bowl, and stir in the remaining flour mixture. Beat well.

Pour the batter into the pan and bake the cake in the preheated oven for 1 hour.

Let the cake cool in its pan on a wire rack for 10 minutes. Turn the cake out onto the rack to cool completely.

Lay the cake on a pretty plate. To serve, sprinkle the cake with sifted confectioners' sugar.

Serves 16 to 20

Note: One tablespoon of cloves is correct.

2 sticks (1 cup) unsalted butter, softened

2¼ cups granulated sugar

5 eggs

3 cups all-purpose flour

1 tablespoon cinnamon

1 tablespoon ground cloves

Pinch salt

1 cup whole milk

1 tablespoon lemon juice

1 teaspoon baking soda

Confectioners' sugar, for finishing touch

APPLE FRITTERS WITH LEMON SAUCE

Western Pennsylvania has many fine apple orchards. Elsie preferred Winesap apples for this dessert.

8 large apples, pared and cored

Orange juice (enough for sprinkling apple slices)

1½ cups all-purpose flour

1½ teaspoons baking powder

¼ teaspoon salt

2 tablespoons sugar

1 egg

1½ cups whole milk

Butter and vegetable oil (for frying)

Lemon Sauce (recipe follows)

Slice the apples crosswise into ½-inch slices. Sprinkle with orange juice.

Mix the flour, baking powder, salt, sugar, egg, and milk.

Dip each apple slice into the batter. Shake off excess. In a frying pan, fry the slices in a mixture of half butter and light oil until browned on both sides. The oil and butter should be at least ½ inch deep; the liquid will sputter but don't cook at too low a temperature. Drain on paper towels. Keep fritters warm and serve with Lemon Sauce (recipe follows).

Serves 8 to 10

LEMON SAUCE

½ cup granulated sugar

¼ cup butter

2 tablespoons water

1 beaten egg

½ teaspoon lemon peel

2 tablespoons lemon juice

In a small saucepan, combine all the ingredients. Stirring constantly, heat to boiling. Serve warm with Apple Fritters.

HOLIDAY SPECIALTIES

Thanksgiving

The Kaufmanns traveled widely and had eclectic European tastes. This was reflected at their holiday table, but some of the Thanksgiving menu was traditional. Elsie Henderson usually made Southern-style Corn Bread Stuffing, and fall apples went into Waldorf Salad with Toasted Pecans. Of course, no menu would be complete without her version of Sweet Potato Pie.

ROAST DUCKLING

Most American families celebrate Thanksgiving with turkey, but the Kaufmanns, who were of German descent, were more apt to have duckling.

Cook the currant jelly, orange zest, orange juice, and minced onion. Add dry mustard.

Preheat the oven to 450 degrees F.

Place the duckling breast side up on a rack. Put in the oven and immediately reduce the heat to 350 degrees F. Roast for up to 1½ hours, or approximately 20 minutes per pound. Baste every 15 minutes or so with cooked sauce.

The duckling is done when a thermometer inserted into the deepest part of the thigh reads 160 degrees.

Serves 2 to 4

½ to 1 cup currant jelly

¼ cup orange zest

1 cup orange juice

1 to 2 tablespoons minced onion

Pinch dry mustard

4- to 5-pound ready-to-cook duckling

CORN BREAD STUFFING

At Fallingwater, the Thanksgiving stuffing was usually baked in a separate pan, rather than inside the bird.

1 cup unsalted butter

¾ cup minced onion

1½ cups chopped celery

2 teaspoons salt

1½ teaspoons crushed sage

1 teaspoon dried thyme

½ teaspoon black pepper

2 cups soft bread cubes

7 to 8 cups corn bread cubes (follow recipe for Corn Sticks, page 59, and bake in cast-iron skillet or buttered 9-inch square pan)

Sauté the onion and celery in butter until the vegetables are tender. Add the salt, sage, thyme, and pepper. Add the cubed bread and corn bread to other ingredients and mix well.

Toss the dressing, then loosely stuff it into the chosen bird. The stuffing can also be spread in a large, well-greased casserole and baked in a 350-degree F oven for 30 to 45 minutes, or until brown.

Serves 6 to 8

Note: To substitute fresh herbs for dried herbs, triple the amount.

SWEET POTATO SOUFFLÉ

Seven miles away from Fallingwater is Kentuck Knob, the home Frank Lloyd Wright designed for I. N. and Bernardine Hagan, owners of the Hagan Ice Cream Company.

Wright did not supervise the construction, but he visited Kentuck Knob, as did some of his apprentices. Edgar jr. was also a guest. Mrs. Hagan wrote a book about her family's experiences working with the famed architect and the pains that the family went to in creating the landscaping that made the most of their house's magnificent setting in the Laurel Highlands.

The home, which was sold to Lord Peter and Lady Palumbo of England in 1985, has a kitchen in the center of the house with a higher ceiling than Fallingwater's, and Mrs. Hagan requested that a skylight be added to provide more natural light. "In our house, I was going to be doing the cooking myself," she said.

Bernardine Hagan loved to cook, and her beautiful soufflé would make a fitting accompaniment to a Thanksgiving turkey or company ham.

CASEROLE LAYER: In large saucepan, peel and boil the sweet potatoes in salted water until tender. Press potatoes through a ricer or mash by hand. (The potatoes may also be boiled in the skins and then easily peeled.)

Preheat the oven to 350 degrees F.

Mix the beaten egg yolks and milk. Add to the mashed sweet potatoes. Mix in the sugar, raisins, nutmeg, and butter.

Spread the potato mixture in a buttered, shallow casserole dish, and bake for 35 minutes, or until light brown on top.

MERINGUE: Beat the eggs whites until foamy. Add the sugar gradually and beat until soft peaks form. Fold in the juice.

Spread the meringue evenly on top of the baked casserole. Place under the broiler for a few minutes to brown the meringue. (This takes only a minute and a half at low broil, so don't leave it unattended.)

Serves 6

SWEET POTATO PIE

In the South, where Elsie Henderson's mother grew up, Sweet Potato Pie usually supplanted the traditional pumpkin pie served in northern states, such as Pennsylvania. This recipe is one of the best, and the Kaufmanns counted on it to highlight fall meals, including Thanksgiving. It departs from the usual recipe, because Elsie sprinkled pecans on the crust before adding the filling.

Preheat the oven to 425 degrees F.

CRUST: With a pastry blender, cut chilled shortening into flour that has been mixed with the salt. Sprinkle with the cold water. With a fork, mix in the water until the dough leaves the side of the bowl. Gather into a ball, flatten, and chill for at least 15 minutes. Roll out to fit a 9- or 10-inch pie plate. Sprinkle the piecrust with pecans.

FILLING: Preheat the oven to 425 degrees F. With an electric mixer, combine all the ingredients, except the melted butter; mix well. Stir in the butter. Pour into

CASSEROLE

6 sweet potatoes (use the lighter-skinned, yellow-fleshed sweet potatoes, not the long, dark-skinned, orange-fleshed sweet potatoes often called yams)

2 egg yolks, beaten (reserve egg whites)

½ cup milk

½ cup sugar

½ cup raisins

1 teaspoon nutmeg

3 tablespoons melted butter

MERINGUE

2 eggs whites (at room temperature)

4 tablespoons sugar

1 teaspoon lemon juice or orange juice

CRUST

⅓ cup vegetable shortening, chilled

1 cup all-purpose flour

½ teaspoon salt

3 to 4 tablespoons cold water

½ cup finely ground pecans

(Ingredients are continued)

FILLING

2 eggs plus 1 yolk, lightly beaten

2 cups cooked yams, pureed

¾ cup granulated sugar

½ teaspoon salt

½ teaspoon ginger

½ teaspoon cloves

1 cup 2 percent milk

⅔ cup cream

2 tablespoons melted butter

the unbaked piecrust. Bake in a 425-degree F oven for 15 minutes, lower temperature to 350 degrees F, then bake an additional 45 minutes, or until set.

Notes: Elsie Henderson warned not to leave out the butter, which "makes the pie shine."

True yams are not grown in the United States; the oblong, dark orange sweet potatoes generally referred to as yams here are actually sweet potatoes. This pie can also be made with the variety of sweet potato that is rounder and dark yellow, rather than orange.

Christmas

Christmas was the time for the Kaufmanns to celebrate with their staff. "This time at Fallingwater is for family," Liliane Kaufmann used to say. The holidays were also an inspiration for Elsie Henderson to pull out some of the family's favorite recipes.

HOLIDAY GROG

Liliane's famed grog was kept warm in the big Cherokee red kettle that swung into the Fallingwater fireplace. This was one potent brew. "We crawled to our quarters after imbibing," Elsie remembers.

30 whole cloves

½ cup light corn syrup

3 cups water

1 teaspoon grated lemon peel

6 cinnamon sticks, broken

2 cups apple cider

1 cup sauterne

2 bottles good red wine

1 cup French brandy

In a large pot, simmer for 15 minutes the cloves, corn syrup, water, lemon, cinnamon sticks, and apple cider.

Add the white and red wines and the brandy. Heat gently. Do not boil.

Makes about 20 4-ounce servings

OYSTER BISQUE WITH JERSEY CREAM

Oyster stew is a Christmas tradition among many European families—especially the English. What made this simple soup special at Fallingwater were the fresh oysters and the whole milk and cream from the Kaufmanns' Jersey cows. Cream rises to the top of milk that has not been homogenized. The heavy cream came from the top of the bottle, the light cream next, and then the whole milk, which was far richer than today's 3.4 percent whole milk. Today the bisque can be enjoyed in a lighter version using whole milk and light cream only, organic if desired.

In a large saucepan, simmer the oysters in butter over low heat until the edges curl.

In a second pan, heat the milk and light cream. Add the salt, pepper, and whole cloves.

Dissolve the cornstarch in the heavy cream. Whisk until smooth. Add slowly to the soup. Add the oysters.

Cook on medium-low heat. Watch carefully to avoid scorching.

Before serving, remove cloves.

Serves 4 as a luncheon main course, more as a holiday appetizer

1 quart fresh oysters, drained

⅓ cup unsalted butter

4 cups whole milk

1 cup light cream

1 teaspoon salt

Dash freshly ground black pepper

8 whole cloves

2 scant tablespoons cornstarch

¼ cup heavy cream

SHORTBREAD TREES

Since the Kaufmanns were Jewish, they didn't erect a Christmas tree at Fallingwater, though they did decorate the house with a few fresh greens. The time between Thanksgiving and New Year's Day was the busiest season at the department store, when sales were higher than any time during the year. So it was truly a time of thanksgiving and a celebration that often included the buttery "tree" cookies baked by Elsie Henderson. The cookies brought back so many happy memories for Elsie that one year she used the recipe on her Christmas card.

Shortbread Trees, winter holiday treats at Fallingwater. Photograph by Linda Mitzel.

1 cup butter, softened
½ cup confectioners' sugar
¼ teaspoon baking powder
¼ teaspoon salt
2 cups sifted all-purpose flour
Colored sugars, for decoration

Preheat the oven to 350 degrees F.

With an electric mixer, cream the butter and sugar until light. Add the dry ingredients, which have been sifted together. Work in until smooth and batter forms a dough.

Roll out on lightly floured board until ⅓- to ½-inch thick. If dough is too soft to roll, chill in the refrigerator. Cut out the cookies with a tree cutter or other desired shape. Sprinkle with colored sugars.

Bake for 20 to 25 minutes. The cookies will be light brown on the edges.

Makes about 3 dozen 2-by-3-inch trees

OTHER SPECIAL OCCASIONS

CHOCOLATE RASPBERRY TORTE

In a latter-day tribute to the changes that have been made in the kitchens of America since Elsie Henderson left Fallingwater, where so-called "convenience foods" were rarely used, here is an easy party recipe she learned to make after she retired. Tasters probably won't guess that it is made with chocolate graham crackers, rather than the rich cake of a typical torte. It tastes complicated but it's not. It makes a nice birthday treat for children.

Mix the applesauce with the raspberry gelatin. (Do not add water to the gelatin.) Let the gelatin mixture stand in the refrigerator overnight or several hours.

Line a 9-by-5-by-2½-inch loaf pan with waxed paper that is long enough to fold over and wrap the top of the torte (plastic wrap works, too).

Make a layer of the chocolate graham crackers and spread with applesauce-gelatin mixture. Continue until the pan is filled.

Fold over the waxed paper and chill overnight.

The next day, whip the cream until soft peaks form; sweeten with sugar and add vanilla. Gently remove the waxed paper and place on an oblong or oval serving plate. Frost the torte with whipped cream. Garnish with fresh raspberries, if desired. Cut into thin slices for serving.

2 cups applesauce, sweetened or unsweetened, depending on taste

1 small package raspberry gelatin

1 box chocolate graham crackers, about 14 ounces

1 cup whipping cream

1 tablespoon confectioners' sugar

1 teaspoon vanilla

Fresh raspberries for garnish

KAUFMANN'S TOASTED PECAN BALL WITH BUTTERSCOTCH SAUCE

For more than 125 years, Kaufmann's Department Store was synonymous with quality and service in the Pittsburgh area. The Kaufmann's clock at the corner of Fifth Avenue and Smithfield Street was a popular place to meet before a day of shopping, which almost always included lunch. Kaufmann's was known for its restaurants.

Jane Citron frequently lunched on the eleventh floor with her mother. The large dining area was partitioned into two rooms, one casual and the other with a more elaborate menu and waitstaff. Her mother preferred the fancier restaurant.

A smaller, more intimate restaurant-café was on Kaufmann's first floor. "Through-

out high school and as a young bride I met friends under Kaufmann's clock, and we went off to the Tic Toc for a bite," Mrs. Citron recalled. "How we loved those hamburgers and toasted pecan balls with butterscotch sauce!"

In 2005, Kaufmann's became Macy's. Though the Tic Toc restaurant still exists at Macy's, nobody could provide the original recipe for this dessert that Pittsburghers will never forget. This recipe, developed by Mrs. Citron, who died in 2007, is based on how she remembered it tasting.

ICE CREAM BALLS

Vanilla ice cream

Coarsely chopped whole pecans, lightly salted and toasted

BUTTERSCOTCH SAUCE

1 cup brown sugar, firmly packed

¼ cup light corn syrup

¼ cup unsalted butter

⅛ teaspoon salt

½ cup heavy cream

1 teaspoon vanilla

¼ teaspoon lemon juice

ICE CREAM BALLS: Form individual balls, about 1 cup each, from vanilla ice cream.

Working quickly, roll and coat completely each ice cream ball with toasted pecans. Place the balls in the freezer on a small tray lined with waxed paper if using within the next few hours. To keep longer, allow the ice cream balls to freeze, then wrap each one in plastic wrap and keep in the freezer until needed.

BUTTERSCOTCH SAUCE: Combine the brown sugar, corn syrup, butter, and salt in a heavy small saucepan. Cook over medium heat, stirring constantly, until the sugar is dissolved. Boil without stirring, 5 minutes or until candy thermometer reads 280 degrees F. Remove from the heat, stir in the heavy cream, vanilla, and lemon juice and cool to room temperature. Store in the refrigerator.

One pint of ice cream will make 4 generous servings. The sauce recipe makes about 1 cup.

Note: A word of caution: If the sauce is kept too long, the sugar tends to become grainy. In that event, heat in a water bath, stirring frequently until the grains dissolve.

BRINGING FALLINGWATER HOME

Seasonal Menus for Elegant Entertaining

Jane Citron and Robert Sendall

Today's hosts seldom have household help (unless they hire a caterer) and they rarely employ a full-time, live-in cook like Elsie. That doesn't preclude entertaining with verve and style. These menus, designed and tested by Jane Citron and Chef Robert Sendall, offer planning and buying tips and do-ahead preparations to execute beautiful parties that will leave guests with memories of great food, elegantly presented.

Jane, who died of colon cancer as this book was coming together, and Bob, owner of All in Good Taste Productions, shared a cooking philosophy that mirrored my own: great food depends on top-quality, seasonal ingredients. It's a philosophy that the supporters of Fallingwater have appreciated. Bob has created the food for more than fifty events there and shared many of his best recipes in this book.

Jane and Bob's menus indicate what cooks can prepare in advance. As a chef and event planner, Bob knew all too well that a few last-minute preparations are necessary, but too many are a recipe for failure. He and his All in Good Taste Productions staff have cooked for gala benefits where 1,100 people enjoyed a four-course dinner. He prepared the intimate meal that the families of Teresa

Heinz Kerry and Senator John Kerry and Elizabeth and Senator John Edwards shared at Rosemont Farms in Fox Chapel, the H. J. Heinz estate near Pittsburgh. That was the day in July 2004 that Kerry announced that Edwards would be his running mate for president.

Decades earlier, Elsie had cooked in the Rosemont Farms kitchen, too—for the late Senator John Heinz's father.

In 1989, Elsie and Bob were under the same roof for Edgar J. Kaufmann jr.'s memorial at Fallingwater. She greeted the invited guests in the house, and Bob created the miniature Reuben sandwiches, cups of tomato bisque, and apple brown betty that nourished mourners on the chilly autumn day.

The memorial food was delicious, recalls Lynda Waggoner. It also presented a particular challenge. The pump went out. There was no water. As an event producer, Bob took the crisis in stride. "After it was over, we were rinsing off our platters in Bear Run," he recalls with a laugh. Talk about communing with nature.

When it comes to entertaining, there are always surprises. At a Friends of Fallingwater event, Bob printed menus for the tables. Some of the courses were French. Following the Cheese Palmiers and the Cold Asparagus Soup was Grilled Poisson with Herbed Oils. The Poisson caused quite a stir. "The next day in Ohiopyle, the locals were talking about how we served possum to all those rich people," Lynda says.

It wasn't possum, of course. *Poisson* is French for fish. The course that followed was a Cold Salmon Galantine accompanied by Vegetable and Potato Skewers. Liliane Kaufmann would probably have loved the salmon—she had purchased a special pan to poach salmon for Fallingwater guests. But when it came to the starch on the skewers, Bob and Liliane would have disagreed. Elsie says Mrs. Kaufmann spurned potatoes, preferring couscous.

Says Bob: "I don't know anyone who doesn't like a potato."

Sweets in the kitchen window: Fresh strawberries, Mint Chocolate Angel Food Cake, Daffodil Cake with strawberries, and tarts.

Photograph by Rob Long.

SEASONAL MENUS FOR ELEGANT ENTERTAINING

When Jane Citron and Bob Sendall created their menus, they adhered to the finest traditions of the nationwide Farm to Table movement. They planned them according to what was available in the season it would be served—in spring, for example, morel mushrooms abound—and used western Pennsylvania producers whenever possible. Cooking and eating close to home makes sense when quality is paramount—the fewer miles something has to be shipped, the fresher, and the better.

Not everyone has the benefits that the Kaufmanns enjoyed—fresh herbs from Liliane's terrace garden, vegetables and flowers from greenhouses on the Fallingwater property, neighbors who offered berries they had picked, and Edgar Sr.'s own Bear Run Farm, which at various times included Jersey dairy cows, beef animals, and lamb. Elsie Henderson recalls Edgar Sr.'s elation at finding Amish farmers on Fallingwater's doorstep to sell their fresh fruits and vegetables and sausage.

Today, America's food traditions are growing richer every day with the proliferations of farmers' markets in urban areas, as well as individual farmers selling produce within yards of where they grew their berries, sweet corn, peppers, onions, or salad greens. Peter Pumpkin-Eater would be well pleased with festivals that celebrate autumn with the succulent squash, in which Bob and Jane found inspiration enough to create a recipe for pumpkin soup in a pumpkin shell.

Chilled Cucumber Bisque, presented in a martini glass. Photograph by Rob Long.

Spring

LUNCHEON IN THE GARDEN

Chilled Cucumber Bisque with Cheese Straws

Classic Salade Nicoise

Tomato and Roasted Red Pepper Tart

Daffodil Cake with Strawberry Compote and Whipped Cream

This elegant seasonal menu may be prepared ahead and served with ease, allowing the host or hostess to enjoy time with the guests. In the early days at Fallingwater, the Kaufmanns would often lead their guests on a morning hike, returning just in time for a refreshing lunch.

CHILLED CUCUMBER BISQUE

2 or 3 Gourmet variety (seedless), or 4 or 5 medium cucumbers, peeled

Butter, for sautéing

1 cup sliced leeks (white part only)

1 bay leaf

1 rounded tablespoon flour

3 cups chicken stock (see note)

1 teaspoon salt

1 cup heavy cream

Rind of 1 lemon, finely grated

Juice of ½ lemon

½ cup finely cut mixed fresh herbs (for example, chives, chervil, mint, basil, parsley, and dill)

Salt and freshly ground black pepper

Cut the cucumbers in half lengthwise, removing the seeds with the tip of a teaspoon. Dice enough cucumbers to provide between 2½ and 3 cups. Reserve the equivalent of 1 medium seeded cucumber for later.

Melt the butter in a large saucepan and sauté the cucumbers, leeks, and bay leaf, covered, over low heat for 15 minutes. Do not brown. A buttered round of wax paper placed directly on top of vegetables avoids browning.

Stir in the flour, then chicken stock and salt. Mix well. Bring to a boil, cover, lower heat to a simmer, and cook the base for 30 minutes. Remove the bay leaf. When the soup has cooled, pour it into the container of a food processor or blender. Puree until smooth. If necessary, puree in batches.

Coarsely grate the remaining cucumber and salt lightly. Add to the base along with the heavy cream and lemon juice. Stir in the herbs, correct seasoning and chill several hours or overnight.

Serves 8 or makes 12 small (demitasse) servings

Notes: In order to properly chill the soup, prepare the base and puree and chill overnight. The next morning, add remaining ingredients and refrigerate until serving time.

Unless cucumbers are in season, use Gourmet seedless cucumbers, which actually are not without seeds, but provide a consistently superior cucumber when homegrown local cucumbers are unavailable.

At one time it was necessary to use homemade chicken stock for soups (see recipe page 49). Today it is possible to buy first-rate commercial chicken broth. Select a natural fat-free brand. Heavy cream adds texture and richness in flavor. Adjust the amount to your diet and preference. Texture and richness may be achieved to a lesser degree by cutting the amount of heavy cream to as little as 2 or 3 tablespoons. The choice is yours. Do not substitute milk. In choosing herbs, select what you like. Mint, basil, and chives work well. Dill may be used alone. The fun in being the cook is to be in charge and make these "executive" decisions.

CHEESE STRAWS

Sift the flour and salt together in a bowl. Cut in the shortening with a pastry blender or blending fork, until pieces are the size of small peas.

Sprinkle 3 tablespoons of the water over the mixture and gently toss with a fork. Push the mixture to one side of the bowl and sprinkle the remaining water over the flour until all is moistened.

Gather up the mixture with fingers and form into a flat disk. Do not overwork the dough.

On a lightly floured surface, roll the dough, rolling from the center, ⅛ inch thick. Using a pastry wheel or knife, cut dough into strips approximately ½ to ¾ inches wide.

Place on a board; brush lightly with beaten egg and milk. Sprinkle with the cheese. Cut each strip into 2- to 3-inch-long pieces. Sprinkle with paprika.

Place the strips on an ungreased cookie sheet and bake in a preheated 400-degree F oven until lightly brown around the edges. Cool.

Makes approximately 40 pieces or more

Note: Cheese Straws keep well in a covered tin lined with foil, and are an excellent accompaniment to have on hand for drinks, soups, or a little snack.

PASTRY DOUGH

1½ cups sifted all-purpose unbleached flour

¾ teaspoon salt

½ cup chilled vegetable shortening (such as Crisco)

4 to 5 tablespoons ice water

TOPPING

1 egg yolk

1 tablespoon milk

½ cup grated Parmesan cheese

¼ to ½ teaspoon paprika

Classic Salade Nicoise, perfect for luncheon in the garden, with Italian tuna, green beans, and Nicoise olives.
Photograph by Rob Long.

CLASSIC SALADE NICOISE

2 small or 1 large head Romaine or leaf lettuce, or in combination, broken into bite-size pieces

½ cup chopped sweet or red onion

1 (11-ounce) jar solid Italian tuna packed in olive oil, flaked

1½ cups blanched haricots verts, or fresh green beans

1 green and/or red pepper, cut into rings

⅓ cup Nicoise olives, or other black olives

3 hard-cooked eggs, quartered

3 tomatoes, quartered

1 flat can anchovies (reserve 4 for dressing)

¼ cup finely chopped herbs (tarragon, chervil, parsley, and basil preferred)

Vinaigrette Nicoise (recipe follows)

Place the lettuce in a large bowl. Add the onions, tuna, green beans, pepper rings, and black olives. Arrange the eggs, tomatoes, and anchovies over the top and sprinkle with the herb mixture. Cover lightly with foil or waxed paper and refrigerate until serving time.

Serves 6 to 8

Notes: For a different look and easier serving, combine the herbs with coarsely grated hard-boiled eggs and sprinkle over the top of the salad and garnish with tomato quarters, pepper rings, black olives, and anchovies. You may vary ingredients according to personal preference, adding, for example, boiled new potatoes, cubed and marinated in olive oil, vinegar and seasoned with salt and freshly ground pepper. Marinade should be added while potatoes are warm. Potatoes are added to the salad with the dressing. Seeded cucumbers and radishes also make a nice addition.

Using premium Italian tuna fish and extra-virgin olive are important ingredients in a Classic Salade Nicoise. The taste and texture of the tuna is remarkable, and excellent quality olive oil provides authentic, delicious flavor. Seared sushi-grade tuna is an interesting option but would not be found in salads on the French Riviera.

VINAIGRETTE NICOISE

With a mortar and pestle, or blending fork, mash the anchovies, herbs, and egg into a paste. Add the pepper, mustard, wine vinegar, and olive oil. Adjust the seasonings, adding salt if necessary.

To serve, arrange pieces of the tomato and egg on plates. Toss the remaining salad with dressing and serve.

Serves 6 to 8

Notes: The dressing and salad may be assembled 4 hours before serving. The dressing should be kept at room temperature and the salad in the refrigerator loosely covered with wax paper. To prepare further ahead, do not cut tomatoes and eggs until ready to serve.

4 anchovies

2 tablespoons mixed herbs (parsley, tarragon, and chervil)

1 hard-cooked egg

Freshly ground black pepper

1 tablespoon Dijon mustard

3 tablespoons white wine vinegar

¾ cup extra-virgin olive oil

TOMATO AND ROASTED RED PEPPER TART

This is easy to make and a good choice for novice bread makers.

CRUST: In a small bowl, sprinkle the yeast over lukewarm water. Add the sugar and proof for 5 minutes. Place the flour in a bowl or on a board and make a well in the center. Add the egg and the dissolved yeast.

Gradually incorporate the flour into the egg mixture with a fork until the dough can be formed with your hands. If the dough seems too soft, add more flour. Turn the dough onto a floured surface and knead until elastic and smooth, about 5 minutes.

Transfer to oiled bowl, cover, and allow dough to rise in a warm place until doubled, 45 minutes to 1 hour.

Punch the dough down on a floured board and roll or stretch it to fit a lightly oiled 11½-inch tart pan. Set aside for 1 hour.

FILLING: Heat the olive oil in a large frying pan. Add the onions and cook over medium heat, stirring often, until golden, approximately 10 minutes. Add garlic; cook an additional minute or two. Add the tomatoes and tomato paste, mixing well.

CRUST

½ package active dry yeast (1½ teaspoons)

⅓ cup lukewarm water

Pinch of sugar

1½ cups unbleached all-purpose flour

1 egg, beaten with ¾ teaspoon salt

FILLING

3 or 4 tablespoons olive oil

1 cup peeled and chopped onions

3 cloves garlic, peeled and minced

1 cup finely chopped tomatoes (4 medium tomatoes)

1 tablespoon tomato paste

(Ingredients are continued)

Tomato and Roasted Red Pepper Tart, easy enough for a beginner. Photograph by Rob Long.

Season with salt and pepper; add sugar, saffron, and bouquet garni. Simmer covered, over medium low heat, stirring occasionally, until most of the liquid has evaporated and the sauce is thick, about 20 minutes.

To bake, preheat the oven to 425 degrees F.

Spread the tomato mixture evenly over the surface of the dough. Cut the red peppers into thin strips and arrange them on top of the tomato mixture to make a lattice pattern. Place half of an olive in the center of each square.

Brush the rim of the dough with egg wash and bake until the tart is lightly browned and cooked through, about 25 minutes.

Makes 8 to 10 servings

Notes: Roast peppers directly over a gas flame or under the broiler, cooking until blistered all over. Turn the peppers frequently. When done, place the peppers in a paper bag and steam for 10 minutes to soften the skin, then peel and remove the core, seeds, and veins.

Alternately, peppers may be baked on a baking sheet in a 350-degree F oven until the skins soften, about 30 minutes.

Tomato and Roasted Red Pepper Tart should be served at room temperature, which allows for advance preparation and a gentle reheating, if necessary. The tart may be assembled a few hours ahead, refrigerated lightly covered with foil, and baked closer to serving time to create a "fresh from the oven" feeling.

Salt and freshly ground black pepper

Pinch of sugar

Large pinch of saffron

Bouquet garni made with thyme sprigs, parsley stems, bay leaf, and tarragon

2 large red peppers, roasted (see note)

¼ cup oil-cured black olives, pitted and cut into halves

1 egg yolk, mixed with 1 tablespoon milk

DAFFODIL CAKE WITH STRAWBERRY COMPOTE AND WHIPPED CREAM

Preheat the oven to 375 degrees F. Place the rack in the middle of the oven.

Sift sifted flour again with the ½ cup sugar.

In the bowl of an electric mixer, beat the egg whites with the cream of tartar and salt until soft peaks form.

Begin at medium speed, slowly increasing speed to high while gradually adding the 1 cup sugar. Beat until stiff peaks form.

1 cup sifted cake flour

½ cup granulated sugar plus 1 cup plus 2 tablespoons, divided

1⅓ cup egg whites (approximately 11), at room temperature

1¼ teaspoons cream of tartar

¼ teaspoon salt

(Ingredients are continued)

4 egg yolks

Grated rind of 1 orange

2 tablespoons orange juice

2 tablespoons sugar

½ teaspoon vanilla

Confectioners' sugar, for dusting

Sift about one-quarter of the flour-sugar mixture over the whites; fold in gently, then fold in remaining flour in three parts.

In a second bowl, beat the egg yolks, grated rind, orange juice, and the remaining 2 tablespoons sugar until the mixture is light in color and slightly thickened. Fold half of the white mixture into the yolks.

Fold the vanilla into the white half of the mixture. Spoon the batters alternately into an ungreased 10-inch tube pan.

Bake for 30 to 35 minutes. Invert pan; cool.

Remove the cake from the pan, place on plate, and dust with confectioners' sugar.

Serve cake with Strawberry Compote (recipe follows).

Makes 12 servings

Note: Baking is not the time to be creative. Follow directions carefully and to avoid a mishap, have ingredients ready before you begin. For example, "1 cup sifted cake flour" means the flour is sifted before measuring. "1 cup flour, sifted" is measured, then sifted.

STRAWBERRY COMPOTE

Strawberries

Sugar

Balsamic vinegar

Remove the stems and any dirt from the berries. If large, cut into halves or slices.

Place the berries in a bowl, sprinkle liberally with sugar, and mix well.

Add a few drops of balsamic vinegar, mix again, and allow the berries to sit at room temperature at least 30 minutes before serving.

Note: Using authentic Aceto Balsamico Tradizionale Vinegar from Modena, Italy, adds a divine flavor and dimension to strawberries.

WELCOME SPRING DINNER

Morel Mushroom Bisque

Roasted Rack of Lamb Persillade

Zucchini Frite with Peppered Yogurt Sauce

These three recipes could be the centerpiece of any spring dinner. They demonstrate how challenging preparations are handled with precision and care. Suggested accompaniments are spring greens, roasted new potatoes, asparagus, and perhaps a simple dish of locally grown strawberries with Crème Fraiche.

MOREL MUSHROOM BISQUE

Wipe the first amount of mushrooms with a damp paper towel. Coarsely chop. If using dried mushrooms, soak in warm water; they will double in size.

Remove and discard the stems and brush off any grit from morels. Reserve 1 cup of the smallest morels and coarsely chop the second cup.

Melt the butter in a deep saucepan or small soup pot. Add the finely chopped shallots or green onions and sauté over medium heat until soft but not brown. Add the garlic and chopped mushrooms. Mix well and cook 4 or 5 minutes, stirring occasionally. Season the vegetables with salt and freshly ground pepper. Add the flour, mix well, and cook 2 minutes, stirring frequently. Add the stock, stir to blend, and bring to a boil.

Lower the heat, cover the pot and simmer 20 minutes.

Remove the soup from the heat and cool to lukewarm, then process in small batches in a food processor with a metal blade or a blender until the soup is very smooth. Soup may also be passed through a food mill. Clean the pot and heat the additional butter.

If the morels are small, keep them whole, but cut the bigger morels into large pieces and sauté in butter 4 or 5 minutes until soft. Season with the salt and freshly ground pepper and add the pureed soup to the pot. Heat and add heavy cream to taste.

2 cups fresh mushrooms of your choice

2 cups fresh morel mushrooms, divided, or 1 cup dried

4 tablespoons unsalted butter

2 shallots, finely chopped (about 3 to 4 tablespoons) or white part of green onions

2 garlic cloves, peeled and minced

Salt and freshly ground black pepper

4 tablespoons flour

4 cups chicken stock

1 to 2 tablespoons unsalted butter

½ to 1 cup heavy cream, or to taste

White or Black Truffle oil, optional

Snipped chives

Before serving, drizzle a small amount of truffle oil over each serving and garnish with a sprinkling of snipped chives.

Makes 8 servings

Notes: The morel mushroom is a harbinger of spring. Native to France, fresh morel mushrooms have recently found a place in the U.S. market and are available from early spring through early summer. Morels add interesting texture to a dish and work well in soups and sauces, where, because of their sponge-like consistency, they absorb flavor. Though expensive, morels are light and a quarter of a pound goes a long way.

Dried morels work in any recipe calling for morels. If using dry morels, use 1 cup instead of 2. These mushrooms require a 30-minute soak in hot water; once reconstituted, they become larger. Remove the stems and clean around the mushroom opening to remove any grit. Opinion differs on whether morels impart flavor to the water in which they are soaked. The water may either be used in the soup or discarded, depending on personal preference.

The addition of heavy cream adds a rich smoothness to the soup. The full measure of cream is more delicious but even 2 to 3 tablespoons cream will make a difference. Do not substitute milk; use minimal cream instead.

ROASTED RACK OF LAMB PERSILLADE

2 whole racks of lamb, trimmed (4 pieces; see note)

SAUCE
Meat and bone trimmings

Butter as needed

½ cup red wine

½ cup Port wine

4 to 5 cups veal stock or good quality chicken stock, divided

(Ingredients are continued)

LAMB: Preheat the oven to 500 degrees F.

Trim racks, removing almost all fat. Clean meat trimmings of all fat and reserve.

SAUCE: Brown the meat and bone trimmings in a small amount of butter in a frying pan. Turn the meat frequently to brown well, being careful not to burn. When the trimmings are brown and crisp, blot dry, then transfer to a 3-quart saucepot. Discard any fat in the frying pan.

Return the pan to the heat and deglaze with red wine. Add the Port wine and deglaze again. Add 1 cup stock, reduce liquid to about one-third, and transfer to a saucepot. Add 2 more cups of stock, bring to a boil, lower heat, cover, and cook at a simmer for 30 minutes.

Rack of Lamb Persillade, centerpiece for a spring dinner. Photograph by Rob Long.

Strain the stock and remove as much surface fat as possible. Pour in a clean frying pan and cook over moderate heat, uncovered, until the stock has been reduced to a sauce-like consistency. At this point, a cornstarch slurry (1 tablespoon cornstarch dissolved in 2 tablespoons cold stock or water) may be gradually added to simmering sauce to thicken to desired consistency.

MUSTARD COATING: Mix salt, pepper, mustard, and olive oil. Paint the racks with mustard coating. Set the racks, meat side up, in a shallow roasting pan and in the upper middle level of the oven. Roast 10 minutes at 500 degrees F.

CRUMB TOPPING: Mix bread crumbs, oil, garlic, and parsley. Lower the oven temperature to 400 degrees F, pat the crumb topping evenly over top and roast 12 to 15 minutes longer.

For a brown topping, place the meat under a hot broiler for a few seconds. Allow to rest 10 to 15 minutes before carving.

Makes 8 servings

Note: Each rack of lamb has 7 or 8 chops. Two pieces equal one whole rack. A high-quality rack of lamb, such as local Elysian Fields lamb, used often by Robert Sendall and Jane Citron, makes this menu a premier meal.

MUSTARD COATING

½ teaspoon salt

Freshly ground black pepper

2 to 3 tablespoons Dijon mustard

3 or 4 tablespoons olive oil

CRUMB TOPPING

1½ cups fresh white bread crumbs

Enough olive oil to moisten crumbs (3 or 4 tablespoons)

3 or 4 cloves garlic, minced

4 tablespoons finely chopped parsley

ZUCCHINI FRITE WITH PEPPERED YOGURT SAUCE

Jane Citron learned this recipe many years ago from Marcella Hazan while attending her cooking school in Bologna. The secret of using water in the recipe keeps the batter light. For less oil saturation during frying, be sure the oil is hot but not to the point of burning the zucchini.

1 pound zucchini

Salt

Approximately ⅔ cup flour, or enough to make a coating batter

1 cup water

Vegetable or corn oil (enough to come up ¾ inch on the side of the frying pan)

Yogurt Sauce (recipe follows)

Wash the zucchini and cut each one into 2½- to 3-inch chunks. Slice the chunks lengthwise into thin slices ⅛-inch thick. Salt the slices and drain for 20 minutes. Pat dry.

Put the water in a shallow dish and gradually add the flour using a sifter or strainer, whisking the mixture to blend. Add salt to taste. The batter should have the consistency of loose sour cream; if necessary, add more flour to thicken, or thin with water. Add the zucchini to the batter and coat the pieces evenly.

Heat the oil until hot but not smoking. Slip in only as many zucchini as will fit comfortably in the pan. Do not crowd. When a golden crust has formed on the first side, turn and brown the second side. Drain on a paper towel and salt lightly. Serve with grated Parmesan cheese, lemon wedges, or Yogurt Sauce.

Makes 6 to 8 appetizer servings

YOGURT SAUCE

1 cup plain yogurt

Lawry's Seasoned Pepper or a coarse ground pepper of your choice

Mix the yogurt in a small bowl and top with seasoned pepper.

Makes 1 cup

Summer

COUNTRY BRUNCH

Champagne Mimosas

Parmesan Cheese Sticks

*Muffin Basket (Banana Nut Muffins and
    Orange Poppy Seed Mini-Muffins)*

Eggs Mornay

Sausage and Cheese Strata

Coffee Service and Cinnamon Palmiers

CHAMPAGNE MIMOSAS

Pour the champagne into each individual fluted glass until half full. Add the orange juice. Do not stir. Serve immediately.

1 quart fresh orange juice

1 bottle champagne

PARMESAN CHEESE STICKS

This is also an excellent accompaniment to shrimp or as a snack hors d'oeuvre.

Preheat the oven to 350 degrees F.

Mix the flour, baking powder, and salt in a food processor. Add the butter and pulse. Add the cheese; pulse again. Add the egg and process until the egg is combined. Turn the contents (it will be loose crumbs) onto a wooden board and gather into a round. It is helpful to do a *fraisage*: Extend the dough in 2-inch smears about 6 inches long until the dough is flat. Repeat and form into a flat disk.

Roll the disk on a floured board or pastry cloth into a rectangle between ¼ to ½ inch. With a pastry cutter, cut into 4-inch strips, ¾ to 1 inch wide.

1½ cups all-purpose flour

3 teaspoons baking powder

¼ teaspoon salt

1 stick cold unsalted butter, cut into pieces

½ cup coarsely grated Fontina cheese (about 2 ounces)

1 large egg

(Ingredients are continued)

Egg wash (1 egg yolk combined with 1 tablespoon milk)

⅓ cup grated Parmesan cheese

Paprika to taste

Place the sticks on a greased cooking sheet. Brush lightly with the egg wash and sprinkle with the Parmesan-paprika mix. Bake 15 minutes. Cool on a rack.

Makes approximately 40 4-inch cheese sticks

Note: Cheese sticks may be served directly from the oven or at room temperature. Vary the dough by adding a different cheese or fresh herbs. The topping may be varied by adding ground toasted cumin, fennel seed, or chili powder with or instead of the Parmesan.

BANANA NUT MUFFINS

1 extra large egg

1½ cups milk

6 tablespoons melted butter, cooled slightly

3 cups sifted all-purpose flour

6 tablespoons sugar

1 tablespoon plus ½ teaspoon baking powder

1½ teaspoon salt

1 cup mashed, very ripe bananas (3 or 4)

½ cup chopped, lightly toasted walnuts

Preheat the oven to 400 degrees F.

Beat the egg lightly with a fork. Stir in the milk and melted butter. Sift together the flour, sugar, baking powder, and salt. Add to the egg, stirring just until the flour is moistened. Add 1 cup mashed banana and ½ cup walnuts and mix only until blended.

Divide the batter between 18 muffin cups, filling almost to the top. Bake 20 to 25 minutes.

Makes 18 muffins

ORANGE POPPY SEED MINI-MUFFINS

Jane Citron first saw this recipe in the Williams-Sonoma Muffins Cookbook *and made some small adjustments. She changed the flavoring from lemon to orange and made mini-muffins—the perfect accompaniment to a brunch or with a Mimosa.*

½ cup butter, at room temperature

⅔ cup granulated sugar

2 large eggs, separated

1⅓ cups unbleached all-purpose flour

(Ingredients are continued)

Preheat the oven to 350 degrees F. Grease 18 mini-muffin cups with butter or nonstick cooking spray.

Using an electric mixer, cream the butter and sugar until light and fluffy. Add the egg yolks, one at a time, blending well after each addition. Sift together the flour, baking powder, baking soda, and salt. Add the orange zest and poppy seeds. On low speed, add the dry ingredients alternately with the buttermilk, blending well after each addition. Add the orange juice and vanilla and beat until just smooth.

In a second bowl, using a clean beater, beat the egg whites just until soft peaks form. With a rubber spatula gently fold the whites into the batter. Spoon the batter into the prepared muffin tins, almost to the top. Bake until golden brown and resilient to the touch. Cool a few minutes before removing the muffins to a rack. Serve at room temperature. Muffins may be reheated later or frozen.

Makes 18 small muffins

1 teaspoon baking powder

½ teaspoon baking soda

¼ teaspoon salt

2 tablespoons poppy seeds

Grated zest of 1 brightly colored large orange

½ cup buttermilk

2 tablespoons orange juice

1 teaspoon vanilla extract (optional)

EGGS MORNAY

This is an excellent dish to serve at brunch or lunch and should be finished in a beautiful oven-to-table casserole so that the finished preparation comes out piping hot to the table. These may be served with assorted grilled sausages.

In a sauté pan heat the olive oil over medium to high heat, and sauté the assorted wild mushrooms until they are browned slightly. Add the shallots and continue to cook until the mushroom liquid has cooked out; reduce the heat. Add the white wine and let the mushroom duxelle simmer until the liquid has been cooked out, about 15 minutes, stirring occasionally. Remove from the heat and let cool.

Prepare the eggs and remove the hard-cooked egg yolks. Place the egg yolks in a clean cotton towel and begin to chop the yolks with a French knife, using the towel to move the yolks around while chopping them. (This is the best way to chop egg yolks. The towels keeps them together so they don't get all over your chopping board, and it also prevents the chopping board from getting covered in smashed egg yolks.) Transfer the chopped yolks to a bowl and fold in the cooled mushroom duxelle. Mix in the fresh herbs and mustard and season with salt and peppers.

Take the hard-cooked egg white halves and generously spoon the duxelle mixture into them, making sure the mixture is nicely rounded on top. Place the filled eggs in a buttered oven-to-table casserole dish. Cover and keep cool. Prepare Mornay Sauce (recipe follows).

6 cups assorted whole wild mushrooms cleaned and finely chopped (cremini, button, oyster)

½ cup olive oil

½ cup shallots, finely chopped

½ cup white wine

10 extra large eggs, hard-cooked, peeled, and cut in half lengthwise

1 teaspoon dry mustard

⅓ cup chopped Italian parsley

⅓ cup thinly sliced fresh chives

1 tablespoon chopped fresh thyme

¼ teaspoon cayenne pepper

Kosher salt and freshly cracked pepper to taste

½ cup fresh bread crumbs

Mornay Sauce (recipe follows)

Eggs Mornay, great for breakfast or brunch. Photograph by Rob Long.

Spoon Mornay Sauce over each prepared stuffed egg, using all of the sauce. Sprinkle the eggs with the fresh bread crumbs and bake at 375 degrees F for approximately 30 minutes. The eggs and sauce should be bubbling hot and the bread crumbs should be browned on top. If not, pass under a hot broiler to brown the crumbs.

Serve piping hot.

Serves 10

MORNAY SAUCE

3 tablespoons sweet butter

4 tablespoons flour

1½ cups chicken stock

½ cup heavy cream

1 cup grated Gruyere cheese

¼ cup grated Parmigiano-Reggiano cheese

Salt

Freshly cracked white pepper

Melt butter in a saucepan and stir in the flour with a wooden spatula. Cook, stirring constantly, over high heat for at least 2 minutes. Do not let the flour brown. Take the pan off the heat and add the stock all at once, beating vigorously with a whisk. Return the pan to high heat and cook, stirring, until the mixture thickens and comes to a boil. Stir in the heavy cream and grated cheeses; cook until the cheeses melt. Season to taste with salt and pepper and let cool slightly.

SAUSAGE AND CHEESE STRATA

This hearty dish is made ahead, refrigerated, and baked the next day.

Brown the sausage meat in a heavy skillet and drain on paper towels, reserving 1 tablespoon fat. Grease a 2-quart soufflé dish or oven-to-table dish with sausage fat.

Layer the bread, cheese, and sausage, starting and ending with the bread. Beat the eggs and add milk, cream, mustard, spices, and wine reduction. Pour over the pudding and finish with the cheese and dot with butter. Let rest overnight.

The next day, preheat the oven to 350 degrees F. Bring the prepared dish to room temperature. Bake until set, approximately 1 hour. Garnish with fresh herbs.

Serves 6 to 8

1 pound sausage meat

1 Pullman loaf (remove crust and cube)

2 pounds grated cheese

8 eggs

2 cups milk

1 cup cream

Salt and freshly cracked pepper

1 tablespoon Dijon mustard

1 tablespoon chopped garlic and shallots (reduced with ½ cup white wine to ¼ cup)

6 tablespoons butter

1 tablespoon chopped fresh herbs for garnish

CINNAMON PALMULLIERS

Frozen puff pastry is widely available in supermarkets, specialty stores, and some bakeries. Using the commercial product has made many classic recipes widely available and turned a once very labor-intensive technique into a commodity that is easy to use and provides excellent results.

Sprinkle 1 tablespoon granulated sugar on the work surface. Mix the remaining sugar, cinnamon, orange zest, and nutmeg in a small bowl. Reserve. Lay the puff pastry dough on the work surface. (The dough should be rectangular.) Spread the butter evenly over the surface of the puff pastry and to the edges. Sprinkle the surface with the remaining sugar and cinnamon mixture.

Beginning with the short sides, roll the dough inward to make the ends meet in the center. Each side should be rolled equally until they meet.

Place in the freezer for approximately 2 hours. Slice into about 20 disks. Place on an ungreased cookie sheet. Bake in a preheated 400-degree F oven until lightly browned and puffed, about 8 to 10 minutes. Remove and serve.

Makes 20

1 puff pastry sheet, thawed

2 tablespoons unsalted butter, at room temperature

4 tablespoons granulated sugar, divided

2 teaspoons cinnamon

Nutmeg, freshly grated (2 grinds)

1 teaspoon orange zest

Summer

PICNIC IN THE WOODS

Grilled Quail Wrapped in Pancetta

Shrimp Remoulade with Romaine and Radicchio "Slaw"

Orzo Summer Salad

Torte au Blette (Savory Spinach and Swiss Chard Bread Tort)

Chocolate Praline Bread Pudding

President Clinton's Cherry Raspberry Pie

GRILLED QUAIL WRAPPED IN PANCETTA

This wonderful preparation of quail is best when cooked fast and served. The pancetta, an Italian bacon, gives the quail a small amount of the fat that is lacking and also adds a wonderful flavor.

4 whole boneless quail, cut in half lengthwise

Freshly cracked pepper

1 shallot, minced

¾ cup finely chopped parsley

½ teaspoon lemon zest

1 tablespoon chopped fresh thyme

1 tablespoon finely sliced fresh chives

12 thin slices pancetta

Olive oil

After the quail is cut in half, remove the wing and make sure that the only bone that remains is the tiny leg bone. Season with pepper.

On a cutting board, place the shallot, parsley, lemon zest, and thyme. Chop until they are finely chopped and mixed together, then add the sliced chives. Rub the prepared quails with the herb mixture and set aside.

Lay the pancetta slices flat and with the wing end of the quail, begin wrapping with the pancetta, keeping it tight as you wrap each quail. (This is important, so the pancetta does not unwrap while cooking.) Keep the quail chilled until ready to cook.

On a flat-top service grill or in a very hot oven (450 degrees F) cook the quail by first drizzling olive oil on the quail and then cooking until the pancetta is crisp and brown. The quail should be slightly pink inside and juicy.

Serves 8

SHRIMP REMOULADE WITH ROMAINE
AND RADICCHIO "SLAW"

SAUCE: Place the egg yolk and the mustard in a small bowl. Begin blending with a wire whisk and slowly add the oil, whisking briskly to make a mayonnaise. Add the remaining ingredients and mix well.

Ample sauce for 1 pound shrimp with some sauce left over

SHRIMP: The trick is to not overcook the shrimp. Cut the shrimp shells with a small, sharp pointed knife or scissors along the top and remove the vein but not the shell. Bring a large pot of water to boil and add 1 tablespoon salt and Old Bay seasoning. Add salt and Tabasco. Add the shrimp in shells and when the water returns to the boil, turn off heat and allow the shrimp to remain in water 10 minutes. Place the shrimp in an ice bath and when cool remove the shells. Blot dry on paper towels.

Place the shrimp in a bowl and coat generously with sauce.

Refrigerate 2 hours or longer.

To serve: Combine the romaine hearts and the radicchio on a serving platter. Arrange the remoulade shrimp on top and serve.

Makes 16 to 20 appetizers

REMOULADE SAUCE

1 large egg yolk (pasteurized egg recommended)

2 tablespoons Dijon or Creole mustard

½ cup extra-virgin olive oil

1 tablespoon white wine vinegar

2 teaspoons paprika

1½ tablespoons prepared horseradish

1 teaspoon minced garlic

¼ cup finely chopped scallions (white part and slender green stems)

¼ cup finely chopped celery

2 tablespoons finely chopped parsley

2 to 3 tablespoons chili sauce (Heinz preferred)

Tabasco sauce and salt to taste

SHRIMP

1 pound raw shrimp in the shell (preferably 16 to 20 per pound)

1 tablespoon salt

1 teaspoon Old Bay seasoning

Salt and Tabasco sauce to taste

Julienne of 3 parts romaine lettuce hearts and 2 parts radicchio, cut in chiffonade to make 4 to 5 cups

ORZO SUMMER SALAD

A few years ago orzo was considered exotic. Globalization has brought orzo to many local supermarkets and it may be used in many ways, but don't forget orzo's original purpose—a pasta, delicious with a touch of butter, freshly grated Parmigiano-Reggiano, and a splash of cream. Summer Orzo Salad may be prepared ahead and refrigerated but should be served at room temperature.

2 cups orzo

3 or 4 tablespoons extra-virgin olive oil

Salt and freshly ground pepper

½ cup basil, cut in chiffonade (cut into thin strips)

2 tablespoons extra-virgin olive oil

2 cups Roasted Plum Tomatoes, chopped (recipe follows)

1 head Roasted Garlic (recipe page 133)

¼ cup water

Cook the orzo in a pot of boiling salted water 15 minutes or until tender. Drain and run briefly under cold water. Drain again. Combine the orzo and 3 or 4 tablespoons of extra-virgin olive oil in a bowl. Season with salt and freshly ground pepper.

Heat 2 tablespoons olive oil in a frying pan. Add the tomatoes and cook 2 minutes. Squeeze the garlic pulp into the tomatoes. Mix well. Add ¼ cup water, bring to a boil and simmer, covered, for 5 minutes.

Toss the tomato sauce with the orzo, blending well. Adjust the seasoning, add basil to taste—enough to provide taste and color—and combine well. Serve at room temperature.

Serves 8 to 10

Note: Orzo is a Greek pasta and an excellent accompaniment to lamb, chicken, stews, and soups.

ROASTED PLUM TOMATOES

Plum tomatoes

Good quality olive oil

Salt and freshly ground pepper

Heat the oven to 250 degrees F.

Cut the tomatoes in half crosswise. Line a baking sheet with Silpat (a French nonstick pad for baking) or parchment paper. Place the tomato halves, cut side up, on lined baking sheet, first cutting a small slice from the bottom of each tomato half. Removing a slice from the bottom stabilizes the tomato while baking.

Brush the tomato halves with olive oil and season with salt and freshly ground pepper. Roast the tomatoes about 3 hours or until lightly browned on top. When cool enough to handle, remove the skin. Store well-covered in the refrigerator.

ROASTED GARLIC

Cut off ½ inch from the top of the garlic. Brush with olive oil; season with salt, freshly ground pepper, and fresh thyme. Bake approximately 1 hour in a preheated 350-degree F oven in a garlic baker or wrapped in foil.

Garlic heads
Extra-virgin olive oil
Salt and freshly ground pepper
Fresh or dried thyme

TORTE AU BLETTE (SAVORY SPINACH AND SWISS CHARD BREAD TORT)

Preheat the oven to 400 degrees F.

Combine the flour and salt in a medium bowl. Stir in the water; add extra-virgin olive oil, mixing until well blended. Knead briefly. Press or roll the dough to fit a 10½-inch metal tart tin with removable bottom.

Wash and spin dry the green leafy portion of the chard, discarding the center stems, and chop coarsely. Repeat with the spinach, removing the stems. Chop leaves.

In a skillet heat 3 tablespoons olive oil and sauté the onion until soft. Add the chard and spinach over low heat; cook until the leaves have wilted. Season with salt and pepper.

Combine the eggs by whisking, then add cheese and blend well. Stir in the chard-spinach mixture. When ready to bake, pour the filling into the prepared tin. Bake until the crust is golden and the filling is firm and browned, about 40 minutes.

Serves 8

Note: Torte au Blette is a family dish from Nice on the Riviera. It is important to use the best quality olive oil and Parmigiano-Reggiano (Parmesan) cheese, since these are the dominant ingredients in the recipe and will play an important role in how the finished product will taste.

Parmigiano-Reggiano should be double wrapped in waxed paper and stored in the refrigerator. For the best texture, always grate it by hand.

PASTRY
2 cups unbleached all-purpose flour
1 teaspoon salt
½ cup water
Scant ½ cup extra-virgin olive oil

FILLING
½ cup finely chopped onion
1 bunch Swiss chard leaves
10 to 12 ounces fresh spinach
3 tablespoons extra-virgin olive oil
Salt and pepper to taste
6 large eggs
1 cup freshly grated Parmesan cheese

CHOCOLATE PRALINE BREAD PUDDING

This favorite dessert has been served at Fallingwater for many events over the years. It can be baked the day before and warmed, though it is best served straight out of the oven. Serve with Crème Fraiche or your favorite vanilla ice cream.

1 to 2 baguettes, cut into 1-inch cubes (generous quart)

¾ cup granulated sugar

1 pound butter, browned and divided (approximately 1 cup in each)

1 teaspoon cinnamon

2 eggs

½ cup sugar

½ cup brown sugar

2 cups milk

2 cups cream

1½ tablespoons vanilla

¼ cup rum

1 cup praline chunks (recipe follows)

1 cup chopped semisweet chocolate

½ cup Crème Fraiche (recipe page 139)

In a large, stainless steel mixing bowl, toss the cubed bread in 1 cup of the browned butter with sugar and cinnamon. Place the tossed bread on a sheet pan and bake in a 375-degree F oven, and toast until dried and lightly browned. Set aside to cool. Lower the oven temperature to 350 degrees F.

In a large bowl combine the eggs, sugar, brown sugar, and ¼ cup of the remaining browned butter. (Save unused butter for another use.)

Add the milk, cream, vanilla, and rum. Soak the toasted bread cubes in the liquid for at least 10 minutes or until softened. Place in a buttered 2½-quart casserole and sprinkle the top with praline chunks and chocolate. Bake at 350 degrees F until a metal spatula inserted in the center comes out clean, approximately 45 minutes.

Check after ½ hour—if the pudding is getting too dark, cover with aluminum foil. When the pudding is browned and set, remove from the oven and set aside. Serve warm with Crème Fraiche.

Serves 8

Note: This can be done in 8 individual 6-ounce soufflé cups.

Chocolate Praline Bread Pudding, a sinful synergy of bread, butter, chocolate, and Crème Fraiche. Photograph by Rob Long.

PRALINE CHUNKS

2 cups sugar

1 cup water

½ cup chopped pecans

Before starting the caramel, grease a heavy baking tray liberally with oil; set aside.

In a heavy saucepot, place the sugar and water and cook over a medium to high heat, covered, until the sugar begins to caramelize. Stir the caramel by swirling the pot slowly in a circular motion. (Do not stir with a spoon.) When the sugar mixture begins to caramelize, add the pecans and swirl them in the hot caramel. Once the pecans have become slightly browned (not burnt) and the caramel has become a dark brown, pour the praline mixture on the greased tray to cool. Once the praline has cooled completely, break it up and place in a food processor and pulse the processor until the praline is in smaller chunks. Set aside for the topping on the bread pudding.

Serves 8

PRESIDENT CLINTON'S CHERRY RASPBERRY PIE

Jane Citron's friend Cynthia Friedman gave a dinner for President Clinton in her Washington, DC, home in July 1998, which Jane attended. She later recalled: "I can attest to no greater thrill than standing in Cynthia's living room and turning around to see President Bill Clinton a few feet away. His magnetism dominates a room." Before the event, Jane made a request through the White House to bake a pie for the president. She was told his favorite pie was cherry, but pie cherries were in short supply at the farmers market. "Making an executive decision, I filled in with fresh raspberries," she said. "I transported the pie with great care on US Airways and then to Cynthia's apartment, where I turned the pie over to the Secret Service. I am not sure what surveillance my Cherry Raspberry Pie experienced, but that evening I stood beside President Clinton as he enjoyed a piece of my homemade pie from Pittsburgh."

TWO-CRUST 9-INCH LATTICE PIECRUST

2 cups sifted all-purpose unbleached flour

1 teaspoon salt

⅔ cup chilled vegetable shortening (she used Crisco)

6 or 7 tablespoons ice water

(Ingredients are continued)

CRUST: Mix the flour and salt. Cut in the shortening with a pastry blender until the pieces are the size of small peas. Sprinkle 1 tablespoon of the water over part of mixture. Gently toss with a fork; push to one side of the bowl. Sprinkle the next tablespoon of water over the dry part; mix lightly; push moistened part aside. Repeat until all the flour is moistened. Gather up with fingers and form a ball.

Divide the dough in half. Form the dough into two disks. Wrap one disk in wax paper to avoid drying out. Roll the second disk to ⅛ inch on lightly floured pastry cloth or board. It should be 1 inch larger than the pie pan or dish. Fold in half, and then unfold over the pie plate, fitting loosely onto bottom and sides. Trim the pastry ½ inch beyond the rim.

Proceed with the filling.

FILLING: Combine the sugar, flour, and salt in a large bowl. Add the pitted cherries and mix well, coating all cherries. Gently fold in the raspberries and transfer to the prepared bottom crust. Dot the filling with butter and cover with the lattice topping.

LATTICE TOPPING: Roll out the second disk of dough and with a pastry wheel or knife cut strips to make a lattice top. Cut strips ½-inch wide and lay enough strips to cover top of pie allowing a 1-inch overhang. Weave the first cross strip through the center. Each time you add a cross strip, fold back every other one.

Fold the lower crust over the pastry strips and press together with thumb and forefinger.

Bake in a preheated 400-degree F oven for 40 to 50 minutes, or until the filling is bubbling and the crust is lightly browned.

Makes 8 to 10 servings

Note: In making a lattice crust, make a generous amount of filling, which allows you to choose the right length of strands of pastry for the topping. For those overwhelmed or too busy to make a lattice crust, it is possible to buy a plastic lattice round at cookware stores that will do the job for you.

FILLING

1⅓ cups granulated sugar

½ cup all-purpose flour

¼ teaspoon salt

4 cups pitted fresh sour pie cherries

1½ cups fresh raspberries

3 tablespoons butter, cut into small dice

ALFRESCO SUPPER FOR A SUMMER EVENING

Thinly Sliced Fennel Cured Salmon with Potato Crisps

Roasted Tomato Soup

Classic Vitello Tonnato with Garnishes
or Bob's a la mode Vitello Tonnato with Garnishes

Fresh Peach Cobbler

FENNEL CURED SALMON

Many years ago Jane Citron attended a cooking class given by Chef Bradley Ogden at Fetzer Winery in Hopland, California. Ogden demonstrated his version of classic gravlax replacing the usual dill with fennel tops. Fennel Cured Salmon has the taste and texture of the smoked salmon. Although the salmon is traditionally served with toast, Jane preferred Potato Crisps garnished with Crème Fraiche and snipped chives.

1 small half of salmon, filleted but with skin on (about 1-½ to 2 pounds) scaled, and trimmed to even edges and bones removed

2 tablespoons cracked black pepper

4 tablespoons kosher salt

4 tablespoons granulated sugar

2 large bunches fresh fennel (feathery greens only)

Combine the seasonings and mix well. Place the salmon, skin side up, on a large piece of cheesecloth and spread half of the seasonings on the skin side of the fish. Top with 1 bunch of fennel greens. Turn the salmon over and top the flesh side with the remaining seasoning and fennel. Fennel greens should completely cover fish.

Wrap cheesecloth over the salmon and place in a shallow pan or on a platter and place a heavy weight—bricks work well—on top. Refrigerate for at least three days and as long as six or seven, turning the fish daily and draining off any excess liquid from the salmon.

To serve: Scrape off the fennel greens and seasonings and slice very thin. Serve with Potato Crisps and Crème Fraiche garnished with snipped chives.

Notes: Crème Fraiche is available at some supermarkets and specialty stores or it can be made at home (recipe page 139).

Keep a pair of tweezers in the kitchen and use them to remove the bones from fish. Run your fingers over the flesh side of salmon to feel and see where the bones are and remove with tweezers. Fennel Cured Gravlax may be frozen and will keep, properly wrapped, for several days in the refrigerator or, if well wrapped, may be frozen.

Consider buying a good quality slicing knife to slice salmon (and other meats or fish) with the ease of a professional. A good knife is expensive but will be a useful addition to your kitchen.

POTATO CRISPS

Scrub the potatoes but do not peel. Grate on the coarse side of a four-sided hand-grater, squeeze out excess moisture, and season with salt and pepper.

Heat the oil in a frying pan, form the potato cakes, flatten, and when the oil is hot, add the potato cakes, frying over moderate heat until brown and crisp. Turn, and repeat on the second side.

Drain the potato cakes, and arrange thinly sliced salmon on top with a dollop of Crème Fraiche and chives.

Note: Keep a pair of tweezers in the kitchen and fuse them to remove the bones from fish. Run your fingers over the flesh-side of salmon to feel and see where the bones are and remove with tweezers. Fennel Cured Gravlax may be frozen and will keep, properly wrapped, for several days in the refrigerator or, if well wrapped, may be frozen.

Note: Consider buying a good quality slicing knife to slice salmon (and other meats or fish) with the ease of a professional. A good knife is expensive but will be a useful addition to your kitchen.

2 large baking potatoes

Salt and freshly ground pepper

Vegetable oil, poured ¼ to ½ inch in a fry pan.

CRÈME FRAICHE

Pour heavy cream in a jar. Add buttermilk and blend well, but do not shake. Cover the jar and let stand in a warm place until the cream has the consistency of loose gelatin. Depending on the heat in the kitchen, this process can be as fast as 6 or 7 hours or as long as 24. Refrigerate for 6 hours before using.

Makes about 1 cup

1 cup heavy cream

3 tablespoons buttermilk

ROASTED TOMATO SOUP

Roasted Tomato Soup may be served warm or cold. It is best prepared when tomatoes are ripe on the vine, usually at the end of the season when tomatoes are plentiful. If you wish to make this when it's not tomato season, use the ripest and best looking tomatoes available. Bob Sendall says that plum, or Italian, tomatoes work best for him.

Olive oil

3 pounds plum tomatoes, cored and halved

⅓ cup shallots, minced

1 tablespoon freshly chopped garlic

6 tablespoons butter

4 large Spanish onions, julienne

1½ cups leeks, julienne

Salt and pepper

3 tablespoons flour

2 cups white wine

⅓ cup cognac

3 cups Pomi brand tomatoes, chopped

4 cups chicken stock

Juice of 1 lemon

Olive oil

Chiffonade of basil for garnish

Pour ⅛ inch of olive oil into a baking casserole or baking tray. Place the plum tomatoes, cut side up, and top with minced shallots and chopped garlic. Bake at 325 degrees F for 1½ hours, until the skins curl away from the tomatoes. (Be careful not to burn the garlic.) Cool; remove tomato skins. Reserve the tomato meat for soup.

In a heavy-bottomed saucepot over medium heat, melt the butter and caramelize the onions and leeks, about 25 to 30 minutes. Season with salt and pepper. Add the flour and cook for 2 minutes. Deglaze with the white wine and cognac.

Add the roasted tomato meat and Pomi tomatoes, and cook on low for 20 to 30 minutes. Add the chicken stock and cook over medium to low heat for 30 minutes.

In a blender puree the soup in batches until smooth. Pass the soup through a fine strainer pushing the soup through with a ladle. Discard the tomato pulp. (Pureeing this soup in a blender will turn the soup a shade of orange. If you wish to keep it more red, use a food mill to strain out the tomato seeds and pulp).

Transfer the soup to a soup pot to keep it hot and season with salt and freshly cracked pepper and a splash of lemon juice. Garnish with basil.

Serves 12

CLASSIC VITELLO TONNATO WITH GARNISHES

Tell your guests you are serving "veal in tuna fish sauce" and they will say "No, thank you." Many are unfamiliar with this wonderful Italian dish, and Bob Sendall never refers to it as that, but as "authentically Italian" and "the perfect dish for a buffet." As with many classic dishes, there are almost as many ways to prepare it as there are chefs. We give you two. This one is Jane Citron's version, and Bob's follows.

MEAT: Make small incisions along the length of the meat with a pointed knife and insert a piece of anchovy and a thin sliver of garlic in each one. In a pot just large enough to contain the meat, place the veal, chopped vegetables, parsley sprigs, bay leaf, and peppercorns. Add enough cold water to cover the meat. Remove the veal and set aside. Bring the water to a boil; return meat to the pot. When the water boils again, cover the pot, reduce the heat, and gently simmer for approximately 2 hours. (If the meat is not entirely submerged, turn occasionally during cooking.)

The meat is done when a metal skewer may be easily inserted into the thickest part of the roast. Remove the pot from the heat and cool the meat in the broth. For easier slicing, the meat should be well chilled before cutting.

TONNATO SAUCE: Combine the egg yolks, tuna fish, anchovies, lemon juice, cayenne, and capers in the bowl of a food processor. Process the mixture into a smooth puree. With the motor running, add the olive oil slowly in a steady stream. Transfer the mixture to a bowl and add heavy cream, if desired. If the sauce is too thick, thin by adding some cool veal stock, a tablespoon at a time, blending well after each addition. Use as much stock as necessary to give sauce consistency of heavy cream.

To assemble the dish, slice the cooled meat into even slices. Trim off any fat or gristle and season the meat lightly with salt and pepper. Spread the bottom of a large shallow platter with a thin layer of sauce and lay slices of the veal side by side. Spoon the remaining sauce over the top, spreading with a spatula. Cover the platter tightly with plastic wrap and refrigerate.

Two hours before serving, remove the platter from the refrigerator. To serve, arrange the garnishes on a platter and top with parsley and capers.

Makes 12 servings

MEAT

3½ to 4 pounds lean, boneless veal roast (in a solid piece and tied to hold shape)

4 anchovy fillets, cut into 1-inch lengths

2 cloves garlic, cut into thin slivers

1 medium carrot, scraped and coarsely chopped

1 stalk celery, coarsely chopped

1 medium yellow onion, peeled and coarsely chopped

1 leek (white part and tender greens), coarsely chopped

6 sprigs parsley

1 bay leaf

8 whole peppercorns

Salt and water

SAUCE

2 egg yolks

1 can Italian tuna (6 to 7 ounces)

5 anchovy fillets

3 tablespoons lemon juice

Cayenne pepper

3 tablespoons capers

1 cup extra-virgin olive oil

2 tablespoons heavy cream (optional)

2 to 4 tablespoons cooled veal cooking stock, if needed

GARNISH

Peeled, quartered tomatoes

Quartered hard-cooked eggs

Italian, Greek, or French black olives

Parsley and capers

BOB'S A LA MODE VITELLO TONNATO WITH GARNISHES

Bob Sendall recommends using tuna fish packed in olive oil for a moist, tasty product. Finding quality veal can be expensive, but it is important to use a lean, solid piece of meat, and remember, the recipe serves 12 persons and even so, you may have some left for lunch the next day.

MEAT

1⅔ pounds tenderloin of veal

Olive oil for grilling

Salt and freshly cracked black pepper

TONNATO SAUCE

4 anchovy fillets, drained and patted

1 tablespoon capers, drained

4 cornichons, chopped

1 tablespoon Italian parsley, chopped

7 ounces Genoa-style tuna in oil

1 cup mayonnaise, homemade preferred

1 cup heavy cream, lightly whipped

Grated rind of 1 lemon

Lemon juice as needed

GARNISH

1 tablespoon capers, drained

Nicoise olives (about 12 to 18)

Chopped chives and parsley

MEAT: Preheat the grill. Brush the cleaned and trimmed veal tenderloin with olive oil. Grill the tenderloin on all sides to create markings and then remove from the grill. Place in a roasting pan and roast in a 400-degree F oven for approximately 10 minutes (do not over-roast; the tenderloin should be medium rare). Remove the tenderloin from the oven and season it with salt and freshly cracked pepper. While the veal is still warm, wrap it tightly in plastic wrap to form a sausage shape. The veal will congeal and hold its shape.

Let it cool slightly and place it in the refrigerator till ready to serve. (This can be done a day ahead.)

TONNATO SAUCE: Using the metal blade in a food processor, puree the anchovies, capers, lemon rind, cornichons, and parsley until smooth. Add the mayonnaise and process just until smooth. Remove and fold in the whipped cream until a thickened consistency. Use lemon juice to thin the sauce to the proper consistency. Fold in the tuna, leaving the sauce chunky. Set aside or refrigerate.

To serve: Cut the veal into slices, place it on a serving platter and pour a little of the sauce over it. Sprinkle with the capers, olives, and herbs.

Serves 12

FRESH PEACH COBBLER

6 tablespoons unsalted butter

1¼ cups granulated sugar, divided

¾ cup all-purpose flour

2 teaspoons baking powder

Dash of salt

¾ cup milk

2 cups sliced fresh peaches

Zest of 1 lemon

Cinnamon for dusting

Preheat the oven to 350 degrees F.

Melt the butter in a 2-quart baking dish. Combine ¾ cup of the sugar, the flour, baking powder, and salt. Add the milk, and stir until mixed. Pour the batter over the butter in the baking dish, but do not stir. Pit and peel the peaches. Combine the peaches, lemon zest, and remaining ½ cup sugar; spoon over the batter and dust with cinnamon. Do not stir. Bake for 1 hour.

Makes 6 to 8 servings

Fall

AUTUMN DINNER

Salmon Rillette

Pumpkin Soup in a Pumpkin Shell

Pork Osso Buco

*Chiffonade of Fresh Beet with Gorgonzola Cheese and
    Toasted Georgia Pecans*

Palm Springs Date Soufflé

Pine Nut Cookies

SALMON RILLETTE

Rillettes are a French preparation made of pork, both lean and fat, cut into small pieces, gently cooked in lard with the usual seasonings and condiments, allowed to cool, and pounded in a mortar. Salmon Rillette is our take-off on the French. The style combines fresh and smoked salmon with a cream cheese base. Salmon Rillettes may be served with croutons, with cucumber slices, or Belgian endive leaves. This mixture freezes well.

Place the salmon in a small frying pan and barely cover it with wine. Cover it with a round of buttered waxed paper, bring to a boil, lower heat, and simmer until the salmon is cooked but still very moist — 5 to 7 minutes, depending on the thickness of the fish. Remove from the heat and cool in liquid. Transfer the fish to a board, discard the skin and any bones, flake the fish, and chop into small pieces.

Put the smoked salmon, cream cheese, dill, and vodka in the bowl of a food processor and process until the mixture is blended. Add the seasonings, then the fresh chopped salmon. Pulse the machine 2 or 3 times to incorporate the salmon, being sure not to over-process.

The finished pate may be served from a crock or piped through a pastry tube onto cucumber rounds or into Belgian endive leaves.

Makes about 2 cups

½ pound fresh salmon poached in

½ cup dry white wine

½ pound smoked salmon, diced

8 ounces cream cheese, softened

¼ cup fresh dill, snipped

1 tablespoon vodka

Salt, freshly ground pepper, and cayenne to taste

Thinly sliced cucumber rounds

Belgian endive leaves

Pumpkin Soup in a Pumpkin Shell, setting the scene for autumn, has been served at events at Fallingwater for many years. Photograph by Rob Long.

PUMPKIN SOUP IN A PUMPKIN SHELL

Pumpkin Soup, made with homegrown pumpkins, was a seasonal fall favorite at Falling-water. For dramatic impact, serve the soup in individual small pumpkins or a large one on a buffet table. Either way is impressive. Pumpkin Soup is best served piping hot with your favorite corn bread.

SOUP: In a soup pot on medium heat, cook the bacon or fat until all the fat has been rendered; do not burn. Remove and reserve the browned pieces.

Sauté the onions in rendered fat and butter until golden, but not brown. Add the pumpkin puree, milk, cream, 3 cups chicken stock, and honey, stirring constantly. Add the ginger, brown sugar, spices, and citrus; heat slowly. Do not boil.

Let simmer, covered, for 45 minutes, stirring often. At this point, check the consistency. If the soup seems too thick, add the remaining chicken stock and adjust the seasonings.

GARNISH: In a small mixing bowl, mix the whipped cream, herbs, and pepper together. Set aside.

To serve: Pour the soup in the desired bowl. Top with the herbed seasoned cream, crispy bacon, and toasted pumpkin seeds. Serve immediately. The cream will melt on the top of the soup and will help finish the soup to a smooth consistency.

If serving in mini-pumpkins, carve out the tops, scoop out the seeds, and clean the insides. Bake pumpkins, with the lids on, at 400 degrees F for 20 to 25 minutes. This will soften the pumpkins so that they can be eaten with the soup.

Serves 12

Notes: If you used canned pumpkin and the soup is too thick, add chicken stock, water, or orange juice to taste.

The soup may be made the day before serving and refrigerated. This intensifies its flavor.

¾ cup bacon, fat back, or duck fat, medium dice

½ cup butter

¾ cup onions, finely chopped

4¾ cups pumpkin puree (canned or fresh)

2½ cups milk

1 cup cream

3 to 4 cups chicken stock

½ cup honey

1 tablespoon crystallized ginger, minced

1 tablespoon brown sugar

¾ teaspoon marjoram

¼ teaspoon cinnamon

¼ teaspoon mace

¾ cup fresh orange juice, plus grated rind of 1 to 2 oranges, to taste

Kosher salt and freshly cracked pepper to taste

GARNISHES

⅔ cup whipping cream, whipped to soft peaks

2 tablespoons chopped Italian parsley

1 tablespoon chopped fresh thyme

½ teaspoon freshly cracked pepper

¾ cup pumpkin seeds, toasted (or pecans, coarsely chopped)

Reserved crispy bacon or fat back

PORK OSSO BUCO

For a change from traditional Osso Buco, which is prepared with veal, substitute organic/ free-range pork. Pork and veal share the same moist texture and delicate flavor. Pork shanks are smaller and make an attractive, less intimidating dinner entrée and cost considerably less than premium veal.

BOUQUET GARNI

2 bay leaves

5 parsley sprigs

6 cloves garlic, smashed

4 thyme sprigs

5 black peppercorns

3 strips lemon rind

MEAT AND SAUCE

8 organic pork shanks, cut Osso Buco style (3½ inches thick)

1 cup flour, for dredging (discard after using)

1 tablespoon kosher salt, divided

2 teaspoons freshly cracked pepper, divided

4 tablespoons unsalted butter, divided

4 tablespoons olive oil, divided

1 cup carrots, small dice

2 cups onions, small dice

1 cup leeks, split lengthwise, rinsed and sliced in half moons

1 cup celery, small dice

1 cup dry white wine

2 cup tomatoes, peeled, seeded, and chopped (about 1 pound) with the juice reserved

1 cup chicken stock

¾ cup red wine

(Ingredients are continued)

BOUQUET GARNI: Place the parsley down first, then the bay leaves, garlic, thyme sprigs, and peppercorns, with the lemon strips on top. Keep the peppercorns encased with the herbs and fold the Bouquet Garni in half and then tie tightly with the string to keep the peppercorns from falling out.

MEAT: Preheat the oven to 325 degrees F.

Season the pork shanks with half of the salt and cracked pepper.

Mix the flour with the remaining salt and pepper and lightly dredge the pork shanks in the mixture. Pat off excess flour mixture. In a heavy skillet over medium high heat, melt half of the butter with half of the oil. Sear the shanks in the pan, being cautious not to overload the pan. Do not shake or disturb the meat. Slowly caramelize (do not burn) the shanks on all sides, then remove them, and place them in a roasting pan.

SAUCE: Remove any blackened pieces in the pan and begin to sauté the carrots, onions, leeks, and celery in the remaining butter and oil for about 10 minutes, scraping up the browned particles that adhere to the pan. Pour the vegetables over the shanks and deglaze the sautéed pan with the white wine. Pour over the seared shanks.

Add the tomatoes plus their juice, stock, and red wine. Add the Bouquet Garni.

Cover it all with a piece of parchment paper, then a lid. Bake for 1½ to 2 hours before checking the meat. Meat should be checked by piercing meat in its thickest part with a fork. If it releases with ease, it's done and tender.

Meanwhile, combine the Gremolata ingredients; reserve.

Remove the shanks from the casserole onto a platter, cover, and set aside. Discard the Bouquet Garni and strain the braising liquid into a medium saucepot. Process the strained vegetable pulp through a food mill and add to the strained sauce. Simmer for about 30 minutes; adjust the seasoning.

If the sauce is too thin, thicken the sauce with a cornstarch slurry (¼ cup cold water mixed with 3 tablespoons cornstarch). With the sauce at a slow boil, whisk in a small amount of the slurry at a time until you obtain a thick sauce. Simmer for a few minutes to cook out the starch.

Return the shanks to a casserole and pour the hot sauce over the shanks. Cover with foil and return to a 250-degree F oven. Braise for another 30 minutes. Remove the shanks to a serving platter and ladle some of the sauce over the shanks. Garnish with the Gremolata and serve remaining sauce on the side.

Serves 8

GREMOLATA

1 tablespoon orange zest, finely chopped

1 tablespoon lemon zest, finely chopped

1 tablespoon garlic, finely minced

3 tablespoons parsley, finely chopped

CHIFFONADE OF FRESH BEET WITH GORGONZOLA CHEESE AND TOASTED GEORGIA PECANS

In a saucepot, place the beets and cover with water; add the pickling spice. Bring to a boil and then reduce the heat to continue cooking the beets until tender when pierced with a knife.

When the beets are tender, remove from the heat and set aside to cool. It is better to let the beets cool in the cooking liquid. Peel the beets and then slice and julienne. Place in a mixing bowl and set aside.

In a small mixing bowl, whisk the olive oil, vinegar, scallions, mustard, and herbs until mixed well. Set aside. Gently toss the beets in the dressing and season with salt and freshly cracked pepper. Place in a serving bowl and top with pieces of Gorgonzola and pecans.

Serves 8

1 pound fresh beets, boiled until tender, cooled, peeled, and julienne

1 tablespoon pickling spice

8 tablespoons olive oil

4 tablespoons balsamic vinegar

2 tablespoons chopped scallions

2 teaspoons Dijon mustard

2 tablespoons sliced chives

3 tablespoons chopped parsley

Salt and freshly cracked pepper

⅓ pound Gorgonzola cheese

6 ounces pecan halves, sprinkled with 1 tablespoon salt and toasted

PALM SPRINGS DATE SOUFFLÉ

The Kaufmanns had a winter house in Palm Springs, California, as does Chef Robert Sendall. They probably would have enjoyed this dessert soufflé, which is made with minimal refined sugar. It's guaranteed to satisfy the sweet tooth with the wonderful flavor of dates.

2 cups milk, divided

⅔ cups chopped dates (preferably Medjool)

⅔ cups flour

5 egg yolks

10 egg whites

2 teaspoons vanilla

Grated rind of 1 lemon

1 ounce butter

2 tablespoons granulated sugar (optional)

Confectioners' sugar, for dusting

In a saucepan, warm 1 cup milk with the chopped dates; simmer until the dates become softened. In a small mixing bowl, slowly mix the remaining cup of milk with the flour, making sure there are no lumps. Once the date mixture has become smooth, slowly add the flour and milk mixture to the date mixture. Continue to simmer until the mixture becomes thick. Remove from the heat and slowly add the egg yolks, one at a time. Whip the date base vigorously until very smooth (there will be pieces of date throughout the base). Before the base cools, whip in the vanilla, lemon rind, and butter. The base can sit at room temperature if used within 1 hour, or it can be refrigerated overnight.

Preheat the oven to 425 degrees F.

Prepare a 6-cup soufflé bowl with a foil collar. Butter and sugar the sides and the bottom of the bowl. In the large bowl of an electric mixer, whip the egg whites until frothy, but not too stiff. Slowly add the sugar, if using, and beat until stiff, but not dry. Slowly fold the whites into the base and pour into the prepared soufflé dish. Place in the 425-degree oven and immediately turn the oven down to 375 degrees. Bake for 50 to 60 minutes.

The soufflé is finished when a long, thin knife inserted into the center comes out clean. Remove from the oven and dust the top with confectioners' sugar and serve immediately. Serve with Crème Fraiche (recipe page 139).

Makes 8 to 10 dessert portions

Palm Springs Date Soufflé, light and lovely. Photograph by Rob Long.

PINE NUT COOKIES

Pine Nut Cookies are almost too pretty to eat, but once you start, these wonderful little butter cookies can be addictive, and will likely become a favorite.

1 stick (¼ pound) unsalted butter

½ cup granulated sugar

1 egg yolk

1 teaspoon vanilla

1 cup sifted all-purpose flour

Salt to taste (¼ to ½ teaspoon)

½ cup lightly toasted pine nuts, divided

Preheat the oven to 350 degrees F.

In a bowl, cream the butter and sugar, blending well. Beat in the egg yolk, vanilla, flour, and salt.

Reserve 2 to 3 tablespoons of the pine nuts and finely chop the rest. Add the chopped nuts to the dough and mix well with a wooden spoon.

Form the dough into small balls, place on greased baking sheet, and flatten each ball with the tines of a fork. Garnish each cookie with a few whole nuts.

Alternately, the dough may be rolled on a lightly floured board and cut into squares with a pastry cutter before topping with pine nuts.

Bake 12 to 15 minutes until the cookies are a pale gold. Remove the cookies from the baking sheet and cool on a rack.

Makes about 35 cookies

Note: Jane Citron preferred the long, slender pine (pignolia) nuts as opposed to the short, stubby ones. This is a matter of personal taste. Whichever nuts you choose, be sure they are fresh (buy from a store with rapid turnover) and store the nuts in the freezer.

Pine Nut Cookies, simple but satisfying.
Photograph by Rob Long.

HORS D'OEUVRE HOUR (WHAT TO SERVE BETWEEN 6 AND 7 P.M.)

Ballontine of Quail with Cumberland Sauce

Roquefort Soufflé in Phyllo Cups with Apple

Thin-Crusted Pizza with Smoked Trout and Horseradish Crème Fraiche

Herbed Gougere Puffs

*Crabmeat Wrapped in Bacon with Soy Plum Dipping Sauce and
    Savory Hot Mustard*

Maytag Blue Stuffed Shrimp with Classic Cocktail Sauce

BALLONTINE OF QUAIL

6 semi-boneless quail, legs and wings removed

1 tablespoon dried cherries

1 tablespoon cognac or Kirsch, heated

2 tablespoons chopped shallots

2 cloves garlic, chopped

2 tablespoons extra-virgin olive oil

1 egg

2 tablespoons heavy cream, more if needed

Salt and cracked pepper to taste

1 tablespoon pistachios, toasted and chopped

½ teaspoon grated orange rind

1 teaspoon chopped fresh thyme

2 tablespoons chopped flat-leaf parsley

Cumberland Sauce (recipe follows)

Place the bowl and steel blade of a food processor in the refrigerator or freezer.

On a sheet of plastic wrap, place 2 quail, skin side down, and flatten with fingers. Remove the thigh meat and fit the quail together to form a rectangle, keeping the meat close together as a continuous piece. Place a second piece of plastic wrap on top and flatten the quail with a rolling pin. Refrigerate. Repeat this process using 4 quail.

Take the remaining 2 quail and remove the meat from the skin and combine with reserved thigh meat. Refrigerate.

In a small bowl, combine the dried cherries and warm cognac or Kirsch. Macerate for 10 minutes, then strain, reserving the liquid. Dice softened cherries.

Sauté the garlic and shallots lightly in the olive oil. Set aside.

Place the quail meat in the chilled food processor bowl and process, pulsing the machine until the mixture is smooth. Add the garlic-shallot mixture and egg and process again. Add the cream to smooth out the mixture and season with salt and cracked pepper. Transfer the mixture to a stainless steel bowl.

Mix in the reserved liquid from the diced cherries with the pistachios, orange rind, thyme, and parsley. Cover bowl and refrigerate mixture. This is called a farce.

Preheat the oven to 400 degrees F.

Lay out the flattened quail. Remove the top layer of plastic wrap and place half of the farce on the meat to resemble a sausage. Fold the side layers of quail meat around the farce and roll in plastic wrap. Freeze. Once the meat is slightly frozen, remove from plastic wrap and tie with string. Rub with olive oil and place in a roasting pan and into a preheated 400-degree F oven. Turn the ballontines every few minutes to create a nicely browned skin. Baking time should be about 10 to 15 minutes. Remove from the oven and let rest a few minutes before slicing. Remove the string, slice into round pieces, and serve with Cumberland Sauce.

Each ballontine should yield 12 slices

CUMBERLAND SAUCE

Place all the ingredients in a small stainless steel saucepot and simmer over low to medium heat. Reduce the mixture to half. Remove from the heat, cool to room temperature and serve with ballontine.

½ cup red currant jelly

½ cup port

½ cup dry red wine

2 tablespoons shallots

Rind of ½ orange, ½ lemon, ½ lime, finely zested

ROQUEFORT SOUFFLÉ IN PHYLLO CUPS WITH APPLE

When the All in Good Taste Productions staff passed the Roquefort Soufflé in Phyllo Cups at Fallingwater parties, guests always looked for seconds and sometimes thirds. This is a satisfying but not filling hors d'oeuvre that is crispy and light. It is the perfect accompaniment to a glass of wine. The Roquefort cheese and apple provide a refreshing finish.

To prepare the phyllo cups, lay 1 sheet of phyllo pastry on a dry surface and brush lightly with melted butter. Repeat with a second sheet of phyllo pastry and lightly brush the top with butter. Cut the prepared sheet into 12 even squares (approximately 3 by 3 inches) and gently press each square buttered side down into one of the mini-muffin cups, being careful not to crack the pastry.

Prepare 24 to 36 mini-muffin tins with the phyllo pastry and set aside. The cups may be prepared ahead; wrap with plastic wrap so they don't dry out.

Sauté the shallots in the 4 tablespoons butter over medium heat until softened but not brown. Stir in the flour to make a roux. Slowly whisk in the milk and

6 sheets phyllo pastry

⅓ cup melted unsalted butter

4 tablespoons butter

3 tablespoons shallots, chopped

3 tablespoons flour

1 cup milk

4 egg yolks

(Ingredients are continued)

1 cup Roquefort cheese, crumbled, divided

5 egg whites

1 Granny Smith apple, finely diced

Salt (if needed) and freshly cracked pepper

Chopped chives for garnish

stir until the mixture begins to thicken. When thick, remove from the heat and add the egg yolks, one at a time, blending well.

Stir in the ½ cup of Roquefort cheese, season with salt and pepper, and let rest. Whip the egg whites until stiff but not dry and fold into the cheese mixture in three additions.

Spoon the soufflé mixture into the prepared phyllo cups and garnish with the crumbled Roquefort and diced apple. Place into a preheated 400-degree F oven and bake for 10 to 15 minutes until the soufflé has puffed and is slightly browned (make sure that the pastry has browned also).

Remove and serve immediately. Garnish with chopped chives.

Makes 24 to 36 phyllo mini-muffin cups

THIN-CRUSTED PIZZA WITH SMOKED TROUT AND HORSERADISH CRÈME FRAICHE

CRUST

1 cup lukewarm water

2 teaspoons active dry yeast

1 teaspoon sugar

¼ cup plus 1 tablespoon extra-virgin olive oil

2 teaspoons salt

2½ to 3 cups all-purpose unbleached flour

Cornmeal for sprinkling on parchment or pizza paddle

FILLING

1 cup mascarpone cheese

2 tablespoons lemon juice

Grated rind of 1 lemon

2 tablespoons fresh horseradish, or to taste

(Ingredients are continued)

CRUST: Pour the warm water into a large bowl, sprinkle the yeast into the water, stir in the sugar, and proof the mixture 10 minutes, or until foamy.

Add the ¼ cup olive oil and salt. Gradually stir in approximately 2½ cups of flour or enough flour to form dough firm enough to knead.

Turn onto a lightly floured surface and knead the dough until smooth and elastic, about 5 minutes. If the dough becomes too soft or sticky, sprinkle small amounts of flour over the dough or add flour to the work surface.

Lightly oil a large bowl with the remaining tablespoon of olive oil. Place the dough in a bowl and turn it in the bowl to coat with oil. Cover with plastic wrap and let dough rise in a warm place until it has doubled, approximately 1 to 1½ hours. Punch down and divide the dough into two pieces. Roll out each piece on a lightly floured board. Brush with olive oil.

FILLING: Mix the ingredients for the filling thoroughly without overbeating and set aside. The filling should be at room temperature.

TOPPING: Spread the mascarpone mixture onto the prebaked crust and bake in a 425-degree F oven until set and starting to brown (approximately 5 to 8 minutes). Remove from the oven and garnish with strips of trout. Return to the oven and bake until the crust is nicely browned and the cheese has set and is lightly browned. Remove the pizza from the oven; let rest a few minutes before cutting. Serve the pizza garnished with capers and chives.

Makes two 10-inch pizzas

3 tablespoons Crème Fraiche (recipe page 139)

Salt and pepper to taste

Olive oil for brushing pizza crust before baking

TOPPING

Smoked trout, cut into thin strips (about ⅓ cup per pizza)

Snipped fresh chives and capers, for garnish

HERBED GOUGERE PUFFS

Bring the water, butter, salt, herbs, and pepper to a boil. Add the flour and beat thoroughly. Cook until dry and the dough forms a ball. Place in a mixing bowl and begin adding eggs one at a time. Once the eggs are incorporated into the dough and the dough is smooth, add the grated cheese. Place in a pastry bag. Using a plain tip, pipe out walnut-sized portions. Alternately, drop by the tablespoon onto a baking sheet lined with parchment paper.

Bake at 400 degrees F for 30 minutes, or until Gougeres are puffed and browned. They should be crisp on the outside and a bit moist on the inside. Serve warm.

Makes 40 cocktail-sized puffs

¾ cup water

2½ ounces butter

½ teaspoon salt

Rosemary, thyme, and oregano to taste

Pepper to taste

¾ cup bread flour

3 or 4 eggs

½ cup grated Gruyere cheese

CRABMEAT WRAPPED IN BACON

Something very good happens when you combine crabmeat and bacon. The crisp texture of the bacon is a perfect contrast to the delicate crabmeat. Using moistened soft bread crumbs binds the mixture. Wrapping in bacon allows the crabmeat to keep its shape. This hors d'oeuvre freezes well.

1 pound fresh crabmeat

1 cup soft bread crumbs

1½ tablespoons dry sherry

Chives to taste

Salt and freshly ground pepper to taste

2 teaspoons dry mustard

Bacon slices, cut in thirds (preferably thick-sliced peppered bacon)

Soy Plum Dipping Sauce (recipe follows)

Savory Hot Mustard (recipe follows)

Combine the crabmeat, bread crumbs, sherry, and chives. Season with salt and pepper and mix gently but well. Mix in the mustard. Shape into elongated balls about the size of small walnuts. Wrap each ball in a piece of bacon. Secure with a toothpick.

Place on a rimmed baking sheet with a rack and cook in preheated 425-degree F oven until crisp, turning once, about 15 minutes. Serve with sauces.

Makes 30 to 36 hors d'oeuvres

SOY PLUM DIPPING SAUCE

1 jar Asian plum sauce

Light soy sauce to taste

Strain plum sauce (determine how much you need by how many hors d'oeuvres you are making) and add soy sauce to taste.

Makes about 1 cup

SAVORY HOT MUSTARD

3 tablespoons Coleman's Dry Mustard

Pinch of sugar

½ teaspoon rice or other white wine vinegar

Water

Combine the mustard, wine vinegar, and sugar in small bowl. Whisk in enough water to make a smooth paste.

Makes enough for 30 to 36 hors d'oeuvres

MAYTAG BLUE STUFFED SHRIMP

What Jane Citron discovered about serving fresh shrimp is that people will eat as many shrimp as are served. She had made these shrimp since she was a bride and considered them an all-time favorite. Incorporating a blue cheese filling introduces a compatible flavor. Any blue cheese works, but today's cooks seem addicted to identifying ingredients with a proper name. Maytag is a delicious blue cheese with a texture that spreads easily.

SHRIMP: To cook the shrimp, make a lengthwise cut through the top of the shell and butterfly the shrimp by cutting along the vein halfway through shrimp. Remove the vein but do not remove the shell.

Bring 3 quarts of water to a boil; add Old Bay Seasoning, then shrimp. When water returns to boil, remove the pot from the heat and let the shrimp sit in the water for 4 to 5 minutes or until firm and white. Drain in a colander then cool under cold running water or plunge into a bowl of ice water for a few minutes. Remove the shell and any remaining vein but not tail shell. Blot dry and fill.

FILLING: Soften the cream cheese and grate the Maytag cheese. Combine the cheeses with shallot and Dijon mustard in a bowl and mix well. Using a metal spatula or flat knife, spread the cheese mixture evenly into the split backs of the shrimp. Dust the cheese with parsley and served chilled with Classic Cocktail Sauce (recipe follows).

Makes approximately 15 shrimp

Note: Any extra cheese mixture may be used to fill celery or endive or sprinkled on croutons.

SHRIMP

1 pound raw shrimp in the shell (16 to 20 to the pound)

1 tablespoon Old Bay Seasoning

Classic Cocktail Sauce (recipe follows)

FILLING

4 ounces cream cheese

2 ounces Maytag blue cheese, or blue cheese of your choice

1 teaspoon grated shallot

1 teaspoon Dijon mustard

½ cup finely minced parsley

CLASSIC COCKTAIL SAUCE

Combine all ingredients and mix well.

Makes approximately 2 cups

1 bottle Heinz Chili Sauce

Juice of ½ lemon

3 tablespoons beet or white horseradish

Dash Worcestershire sauce

Tabasco sauce to taste

Onion Tart from Alsace uses a crust made in the food processor. Photograph by Rob Long.

Winter

WINTER BUFFET BY THE FIRE

Onion Tart from Alsace

Beef Daube with Porcini Mushrooms

*Winter Salad with Belgian Endive, Haricots Verts, and Toasted Hazelnuts,
   served with Lemon Vinaigrette*

Poached Pears with Saffron and Crème Anglaise

Jane's Mother's Sour Cream Cookies

ONION TART FROM ALSACE

Heat the oil and butter in a large nonstick frying pan, add onions, and cook slowly over low heat until the onions are soft and begin to brown, about 20 minutes. Add water and cook an additional 10 minutes until the onions are lightly browned and caramelized.

Beat the eggs in a large bowl. Combine with the Fromage Blanc and cream, whisking until smooth. Season with salt, pepper, and nutmeg. Add the onions and mix well. Pour the mixture into a prepared pastry shell and bake in a preheated 400-degree F oven for 45 to 50 minutes, or until the crust is browned and the filling has lightly browned and puffed.

Serve the tart at room temperature, allowing it to rest 15 to 20 minutes before cutting.

Makes 10 servings

Note: To make the Fromage Blanc, combine equal parts of plain yogurt with low-fat ricotta cheese. Pass through a fine strainer and store in refrigerator 24 hours before using.

1 recipe Pate Brisee Pastry crust (recipe follows), rolled ⅛ inch thick to fit 11½-inch tart pan

3 large onions, peeled and sliced (about 10 cups, loosely packed)

2 tablespoons butter

1 tablespoon vegetable oil

¼ cup water

3 eggs

1 cup Fromage Blanc (see note)

½ cup heavy cream

Salt

Freshly ground pepper

A pinch of nutmeg (to taste)

PATE BRISEE PASTRY

For many years, Jane Citron said she avoided using the food processor when making a pastry crust. She made her mother's original Crisco crust by hand. In her classes, students told her how they used the processor for "everything"—pasta, piecrust, pizza. One day, for some unknown reason, she tried the Pate Brisee in the food processor. She became a believer. Not only did she save time but avoided excess handling of the dough, which makes a heavy crust. You are never too old to learn.

11½-inch tart pan

1¼ cups sifted unbleached all-purpose flour

½ teaspoon salt

8 tablespoons chilled unsalted butter, cut in small cubes

3 or 4 tablespoons ice water

Combine the flour and salt in the bowl of a food processor. Add the butter cubes and pulse the machine 12 to 15 times, or until the butter is coated with flour and forms particles the size of peas and resembles very rough sand.

With the motor running, add 3 tablespoons water. Stop processing before the dough forms a ball. Turn the dough (there will be pieces) onto a floured surface, and if very dry, add a little more water. Form it into a ball by taking the dough in one hand; using the dough ball as a mop, gathering the loose particles on the counter.

With your wrist flat on the counter, extend your hand upward at a 45-degree angle and with the heel of your hand, slide the dough 6 to 8 inches forward only. When all the dough has been used, reform it into a ball and repeat the operation. This is the final blending. Flatten the dough into a disk, wrap it in wax paper, and refrigerate 30 minutes before using.

To roll the pastry, flatten the dough with a rolling pin and roll on a lightly floured board or cloth to ⅛ inch. Fold the dough in half, lift carefully and fit the dough into the tart pan, trimming the excess dough from around the rim, leaving about a ½ inch hanging over. Turn the crust under and level the top rim with a rolling pin or your fingers.

At this point, the crust may be filled and baked or lined with foil and filled with dried beans and used as a baked shell. When baking a shell, bake 10 minutes in a preheated 450-degree F oven, lower heat to 400 degrees F, remove the foil and beans and finish baking 10 minutes or until golden. This is called blind baking.

BEEF DAUBE WITH PORCINI MUSHROOMS

Daube is a French cooking term describing a method of cooking meat. Although this method can be used for other meat, poultry, or game, that term by classic definition describes a cut of beef cooked in daube or braised in stock generally with red wine enriched with vegetables and seasoned with herbs.

Salt the meat generously. Melt the butter and oil together in a large frying pan and when just about sizzling add the meat in batches (do not crowd) and brown it evenly over medium high heat. Transfer the browned meat to a large heat-proof casserole or pot.

Pour the fat from the frying pan and deglaze it with the first cup of red wine, scraping the bottom of the pan with a wooden spoon to loosen the brown bits. Reduce by one-half and add to the meat. Wipe the pan and add 1 tablespoon additional butter and 2 tablespoons additional olive oil when the pan is hot; add all the vegetables but the tomatoes and sauté 5 minutes. Add the tomatoes, cook an additional minute or two, then stir in the flour, blending well. Add the second cup of wine and 2 cups of the stock. Cook until the mixture boils, then add to the meat.

With the remaining cup of stock, deglaze the frying pan and reduce to 3 to 4 tablespoons. Add this to the meat with the Bouquet Garni and bring the casserole to a boil. Lower the heat and simmer, covered, for 1 hour or until the meat is tender.

Remove the dried mushrooms from the soaking liquid and rinse well. Add the mushrooms after 1 hour and cook 20 to 30 minutes more. Adjust the seasoning and serve.

Makes 8 servings

Notes: Daube may be prepared well in advance and reheated.

The best dried mushrooms come from Europe, especially France and Italy. Stored dry—never in the freezer or refrigerator—in a cool place away from the light, these mushrooms will keep many months. The soaking liquid from porcini may be filtered through a paper towel and added to the daube as part of the cooking liquid if desired.

Salt

3-pound trimmed beef chuck roast, cut into 1-inch pieces

1 tablespoon unsalted butter (more if needed)

1 tablespoon extra-virgin olive oil (more if needed)

1 cup dry red wine

1½ cups chopped onions

1 cup peeled and chopped carrots

1 tablespoon minced garlic

½ cup celery, stringed and diced

1 cup ripe tomatoes, peeled, seeded and coarsely chopped, or equivalent of good quality imported canned Italian plum tomatoes (La Valle or La Bella)

1 additional cup dry red wine

3 cups veal stock or good quality fat-free chicken stock, divided

Bouquet Garni (1 bay leaf and 2 sprigs of flat-leaf parsley and thyme)

3 tablespoons flour

1 ounce dried porcini mushrooms soaked in 1½ cups hot water

WINTER SALAD WITH BELGIAN ENDIVE, HARICOTS VERTS, AND TOASTED HAZELNUTS

Bob and Jane used this recipe in one of their cooking classes. Jane received many compliments on the Lemon Vinaigrette. Using grated lemon rind adds just the right amount of fresh lemon flavor. Salad components may be assembled early in the day, but the hazelnuts should be added with the dressing when the salad is ready to be served.

4 to 5 small heads of Bibb lettuce, in bite-size pieces

4 pieces Belgian endive

½ pound haricots verts (or small, tender green beans), tailed

1 large roasted red pepper, cut into julienne

Mache or watercress

Snipped fresh chives

½ cup blanched and toasted hazelnuts, coarsely chopped

Lemon Vinaigrette (recipe follows)

Place the Bibb lettuce and Belgian endive pieces in a large salad bowl.

Blanch the green beans in a 4-quart pot of boiling and salted water for 2 minutes or until almost tender but still firm to the bite. Drain and plunge into a bowl of ice water for 4 to 5 minutes, drain, and dry on toweling.

Scatter the beans on top of the greens, add julienne roasted red pepper. Top with 2 cups Mache or watercress leaves. Garnish with the chives and scatter the hazelnuts over the top. If desired, hazelnuts may be warmed in a toaster oven or regular oven. Toss with Lemon Vinaigrette and serve.

Makes 8 servings

LEMON VINAIGRETTE

1 tablespoon minced shallots

1 teaspoon Dijon mustard

Salt and freshly ground pepper to taste

2 teaspoons grated lemon rind

1 tablespoon sherry wine vinegar

½ teaspoon balsamic vinegar

2 tablespoons walnut oil

2 tablespoons extra-virgin olive oil

4 tablespoons light vegetable oil

Touch of heavy cream (optional)

Combine the shallots, mustard, salt, freshly ground pepper, and lemon rind in a small bowl.

Whisk in the oils and vinegars, blending well. If desired, the dressing may be finished with a splash of heavy cream.

Note: The best walnut oil comes from France. The taste is excellent, and it is worth seeking out the genuine product. Nut oils have a long shelf life if kept under refrigeration. On the other hand, olive oil should be kept at room temperature in a dry, cool place.

Poached Pear with Saffron, just right for guests in danger of skipping dessert. Photograph by Rob Long.

POACHED PEARS WITH SAFFRON

These richly tinted pears, a favorite of Fallingwater guests, are the perfect dessert for winter and the holidays. It's a regal sculptural dessert garnished with pomegranates.

6 firm ripe pears (Bartlett or Anjou)

5 cups white wine

1½ cups sugar

3 whole cloves

1 cinnamon stick

4 whole allspice

10 threads saffron

6 tablespoons diced dried fruits (cherries, cranberries, apricots)

3 tablespoons chopped roasted pecans

6 tablespoons pomegranate seeds, for garnish

Crème Anglaise (recipe follows)

Peel the pears; core them from the bottom so as not to disturb the stem (leave the stem intact). Cut a thin slice off the bottom so the pear will stand tall. In a pot large enough to fit the pears, combine the wine and sugar and bring to a boil. Stir to make sure that all the sugar has dissolved. Add the spices and simmer for about 15 minutes to infuse the flavors into the poaching liquid. The saffron color will become intense. Poach the pears in the syrup, uncovered, until just tender, approximately 5 to 10 minutes.

Let the pears cool in the poaching liquid and refrigerate until needed.

Remove the pears from the poaching liquid and set on paper towels to drain. In a small mixing bowl combine the dried fruit and pecans.

Fill the core of the pears with approximately 1½ tablespoons of the fruit mixture and set aside for service. In a saucepot return the poaching liquid and boil until the liquid has reduced in half and has thickened to the consistency of syrup (a thicker syrup is always better for this presentation).

CRÈME ANGLAISE

½ cup egg yolks (save whites for another use)

½ cup granulated sugar

2 cups milk

½ fresh vanilla bean, split in half lengthwise

In a bowl combine the egg yolks and sugar; beat until thick and light. In the top of a double boiler scald the milk with the vanilla bean. Slowly add the hot milk to the egg-sugar mixture, whisking constantly. Whisk until smooth.

Return the mixture to the double boiler and stir with a wooden spoon until the mixture coats the spoon, 10 to 15 minutes. Remove from the heat, discard the vanilla bean, and strain the mixture through a fine sieve into a cool glass bowl. This procedure will strain out any lumps and will stop the sauce from cooking. Cover and cool in the refrigerator.

Pour a small portion of the sauce on the serving plate and coat the plate with the sauce by tilting the plate until covered. Place a stuffed pear in the middle of each plate and garnish with the pomegranate seeds. Serve chilled or at room temperature. Serve the thickened syrup on the side for added sweetness if desired.

Serves 6

JANE'S MOTHER'S SOUR CREAM COOKIES

Jane Citron's mother excelled in baking, and she frequently made these cookies, which her family loved. The recipe came from "Aunt" Jessie, who was not really Jane's aunt but a good friend of her mother's. Aunt Jessie said the recipe came with her mother's family from Hungary.

Cream the butter in the bowl of an electric mixer. Add the sugar slowly, beating until light. Add the egg yolks, sour cream, vanilla, and lemon juice. Blend well. Add the dry ingredients and blend again. Gather into a disk and wrap in plastic wrap and chill several hours or overnight.

When ready to roll the cookies, soften the dough at room temperature for 20 minutes before using. Divide the dough into three pieces and, one piece at a time, roll on a floured board or cloth, ⅛ inch thick and cut with cookie cutter. Place on cookie sheet (it is not necessary to grease). Brush the tops of the cookies with the egg white and sprinkle lightly with sugar-cinnamon and chopped nuts.

Bake in a preheated 350-degree F oven for 10 to 12 minutes or until edges are lightly browned.

Cool cookies on rack.

Makes 4 to 6 dozen (depending on size)

Note: Make thin, delicate cookies using a small—not miniature—cookie cutter. You can freeze half of the dough which allows you to have access to a batch of freshly baked cookies.

1 cup unsalted butter, at room temperature

¾ cup granulated sugar

2 egg yolks

½ cup sour cream

1 teaspoon vanilla

1 teaspoon lemon juice

3 cups sifted all-purpose flour

½ teaspoon baking powder

2 egg whites, beaten to blend

3 tablespoons granulated sugar mixed with ½ teaspoon cinnamon

⅓ cup finely chopped walnuts

The Café at Fallingwater in the Visitor Center. Photograph courtesy of Western Pennsylvania Conservancy.

A TASTE OF FALLINGWATER

Recipes from the Café at Fallingwater

As architect Frank Lloyd Wright would have wanted it, Fallingwater remains faithful to its time and place. The Western Pennsylvania Conservancy has kept the house's spectacular woodland setting as beautiful as the first day Wright glimpsed the Bear Run waterfall rush over the rocks.

Visitors who experience what Lynda Waggoner, director of Fallingwater and vice president of the Western Pennsylvania Conservancy, calls the "ah-ha!" moment when they first see the house, know why the National Geographic Traveler magazine named it one of fifty "Places of a Lifetime."

Today, the Visitor Center welcomes guests in a beautiful pavilion in the woods that includes a café and gift shop. Designed by Edgar Kaufmann jr.'s longtime companion, Paul Mayen, the center was completed in 1980.

Memories abound in the 1,500-plus acres given to the Conservancy by Edgar jr., even from before there was a Fallingwater. Dorothy Hay Dull, a local resident, remembers swimming under the falls at Bear Run before the house was built. She was eight or nine at the time, and she'd ride up there on her Shetland pony, Patsy, with the family collie, Laddie. She tied her pony to a sapling and swam in the creek with her siblings. "We wore old clothes," she recalled. "We couldn't afford a bathing suit."

The late Ruth Burnsworth Rugg McVay recalled the days of the Kaufmanns' summer camp, and the young women hiking up the valley along the creek to her grandmother's. An accomplished country cook, her grandmother would "butcher chickens, and bake pies, and make mashed potatoes, and cottage cheese, and have the best dinner you ever saw. They would sit around the little summer cabin where most of the cooking, canning, and drying of fruits and vegetables was done."

Looking back, the area's food was the farm-to-table movement personified. Remembered Virginia Friend Kessler: "The Pittsburgh people liked their fresh stuff; it could be butter, it could be anything. My mother would even mail eggs to Pittsburgh in metal boxes."

Today's fare at the Café at Fallingwater carries on that tradition of farm-to-table freshness and quality. When Mary Anne Moreau, former chef at the Café at Fallingwater, was asked for some favorite recipes, she called for "free-range eggs," as well as the fruits and berries that grow so well in western Pennsylvania. For seven and one-half years, she created a delicious array of soups, sandwiches, and pastries for the Café's visitors.

Reared in Uniontown, Pennsylvania, Mary Anne showed her stuff as a graduate of the International Culinary Academy in Pittsburgh, now a part of Pennsylvania Culinary. She did her externship at another historic site, the Stone House Restaurant and Inn in Farmington, Pennsylvania.

She loved her work in the Café, and praises the congenial staff, including her appreciative boss, Lynda Waggoner. Mary Anne moved to Virginia in July 2006 after her husband took a new job there, but fondly recalls her days at Fallingwater. "It was the most beautiful place to work," she says. "It was a perfect job."

Mary Anne's skill with pastries is evident in the recipes she shares here, and the Certified Sous Chef also created some dinners served at Fallingwater. Those special events continue today under the direction of Tom Shuttlesworth, whose meals emphasize grass-fed beef and locally grown fruits and vegetables. Fallingwater's annual Twilight Tour features wine and cheese in the house followed by a picnic in the meadow with jazz music. There are also Sunday brunches and special lunches on the terrace. A new event is the Sunset Tour, which includes light hors d'oeuvres on the pottery terrace.

Edgar Kaufmann Sr. and his son, Edgar jr., may have disagreed about some things, but they were in accord on Fallingwater: it should be shared with the public. As Liliane Kaufmann once wrote to Frank Lloyd Wright, "Living in a house built by you has been my one education."

Lemon Cake with Chèvre and Fresh Berries from Mary Anne Moreau's Café collection. Photograph by Linda Mitzel.

RECIPES FROM THE CAFÉ AT FALLINGWATER

Fallingwater hasn't lost its lure. Visitors today range from schoolchildren to Elder-hostel seniors to movie stars such as Tom Hanks, Ron Howard, and Dennis Miller. Actress Angelina Jolie took Brad Pitt to Fallingwater as a surprise for his birthday. Fallingwater was gowned in snow when they sipped champagne and dined on caviar that she had shipped to the site.

FUNNY MUFFINS

Today's visitors to Fallingwater will find one Kaufmann tradition still in place. There is always an array of breads to enjoy, as well as plenty of places to hike on the Western Pennsylvania Conservancy land. Former Café chef Mary Anne Moreau calls these spicy coffee cake muffins "Funny Muffins" because they rise around the edges and sink slightly in the middle. They are delicious with coffee or tea.

¾ cup white sugar

¾ cup brown sugar

2½ cups all-purpose flour

½ teaspoon salt

½ teaspoon cinnamon

¼ teaspoon ginger

¾ cup butter, melted and cooled

1½ teaspoons cinnamon

1 cup chopped pecans

1 teaspoon baking soda

1 teaspoon baking powder

1 egg

1 cup buttermilk

Preheat the oven to 350 degrees F. Mix the sugars, flour, salt, ½ teaspoon cinnamon, ginger, and butter in a large mixer bowl until well blended. Remove ½ cup and add to it the 1½ teaspoons cinnamon and pecans. Set aside to use as the crumb topping.

To the remaining mixed ingredients (still in the bowl), add the baking soda, baking powder, egg, and buttermilk. Mix just until the ingredients are combined.

Pour spoonfuls of the batter into greased muffin cups (about ½ to ¾ full). Sprinkle the topping mixture over the tops of the muffins.

Bake for 15 to 20 minutes. Test with a toothpick, which should come out clean.

Makes about 2 dozen

CAFÉ AT FALLINGWATER TOMATO BISQUE

For winter visitors to Fallingwater, this hot soup cuts the chill. It is especially appropriate when local tomatoes are not in season, and it tastes delicious even made with canned tomatoes. Mary Anne Moreau says she always made a large pot, and seasonings are as adjustable as the amount of cream.

4 tablespoons butter

½ cup onion, cut into medium dice

1 tablespoon fresh dillweed, chopped

1 tablespoon Provencal Herbs with lavender

(Ingredients are continued)

In a large soup pot, sauté the onion, dillweed, and Provencal Herbs in butter for about 8 minutes, stirring constantly. Add the flour and stir.

Add the crushed tomatoes, tomato sauce, and stock. Bring to a simmer, stirring occasionally.

Add the honey, cream, half and half, salt, and pepper. Add a few shakes of pepper sauce to taste. (Five is good.)

Makes 8 to 10 generous servings

Note: Adjust the seasonings, as desired. The chef made a larger pot and this was her scaled-down version. To make a vegan soup, use margarine or oil instead of butter, use the vegetable stock, and omit the heavy cream and half and half. "It is very good and lower in calories, too," Mary Anne says.

3 tablespoons flour

28-ounce can crushed tomatoes

28-ounce can tomato sauce

28-ounce can chicken or vegetable stock

2 tablespoons honey

1 cup heavy cream

½ cup half and half

Salt and freshly ground pepper

Few shakes of hot pepper sauce, such as Tabasco

THREE BERRY COBBLER

Western Pennsylvania has a reputation as a great place to grow berries. This cobbler recipe provided by Mary Anne makes wonderful use of those berries—even when they aren't in season. A good way to freeze any extra berries is to lay them in a single layer, unwashed, on a jellyroll pan. Freeze. Pour them into a heavy-duty freezer bag, label with the date, and place in the freezer. When ready to use, pour out the amount required by the recipe (immediately return the rest to the freezer). Rinse and hull (or pit, in the case of cherries) the berries, which will be thawed by the cold water. Lay on paper towels to partially dry.

FILLING: Mix the sugar, cornstarch, and cinnamon in large bowl. Add the berries, stir together gently and pour into a 2-quart baking dish or 9-by-13-inch pan. Sprinkle with the lemon juice and dot with pieces of the butter.

TOPPING: Mix the butter and sugar in a mixer until fluffy. Add the combined dry ingredients and the buttermilk. Mix to combine. The batter will be stiff. Spoon the batter over the berries. The berries will not be totally covered with the batter.

Bake at 350 degrees F for about 50 minutes. The pastry should be brown and fruit bubbling. The cobbler can be served warm, at room temperature, or chilled.

It's good with freshly whipped cream or vanilla ice cream and a sprinkle of cinnamon and mint leaf for garnish.

Serves 6 to 8

FILLING

2 cups each of (fresh or frozen) blackberries, red raspberries, and blueberries (also good with strawberries, cherries, and boysenberries)

1 cup sugar

2 tablespoons cornstarch

¼ teaspoon cinnamon

2 tablespoons fresh lemon juice

2 tablespoons butter

TOPPING

½ cup butter

½ cup brown sugar

1 cup unbleached all-purpose flour

2 teaspoons baking powder

¼ teaspoon salt

½ cup buttermilk

LEMON CAKES WITH CHÈVRE AND FRESH BERRIES

This recipe is another delectable showcase for fresh berries. It tastes surprisingly light and looks gorgeous.

8 ounces chèvre (goat cheese), at room temperature

8 ounces cream cheese, at room temperature

1¼ cups granulated sugar

¼ cup unbleached all-purpose flour

Zest of 1 large lemon

4 free-range eggs, separated

Whipped cream and mint, for garnish

Preheat the oven to 350 degrees F. Butter 6 mini-Bundt cake pans.

With a rubber spatula, mix the chèvre, cream cheese, sugar, flour, zest, and egg yolks. Beat the egg whites until soft peaks form. Fold the beaten whites into cheese mixture.

Fill the buttered mini-Bundt cake pans ⅔ full. Bake from 20 to 25 minutes. Cool for 10 minutes and gently tip out of the pan. Cool completely before serving (also good chilled). Top with fresh berries and dollop of whipped cream and mint leaf.

Note: These cakes can also be made in regular or mini-muffin pans—of course, this is a smaller portion and not nearly as impressive as a personal Bundt cake.

HONEY MAPLE PECAN BARS

This was one of Mary Anne Moreau's favorite sweets, and director Lynda Waggoner recommends it, too. It makes a lot, so it would be great for a neighborhood supper or family reunion.

PASTRY

1½ cups chilled butter

1 cup confectioners' sugar

4 cups unbleached all-purpose flour

2 large free-range eggs

FILLING

1½ cups brown sugar, packed

½ cup honey

¼ cup pure maple syrup

¾ cup chilled butter

1 tablespoon vanilla extract

4 cups pecan halves or pieces

Preheat the oven to 375 degrees F.

CRUST: Combine the 1½ cups butter and confectioners' sugar in a food processor. Pulse 20 seconds. Add the eggs and flour and process just until a dough forms. Press the dough onto the bottom of a half-sheet pan (see note) and halfway up the sides. Bake 15 to 20 minutes or until golden. Cool slightly.

FILLING: Bring the brown sugar, honey, maple syrup, and the remaining ¾ cup butter to a boil. Stir frequently, and boil exactly 2 minutes. Take off the heat and add the pecans and vanilla. Pour into the baked pastry crust, spread with a spatula, and return to the oven and bake an additional 20 minutes. The top should be bubbly. Remove from the oven, cool, and cut into bars.

Note: A half-sheet pan is a size commonly used in commercial kitchens. If you don't have one, an approximate substitution would be a 15½-by-10½-inch jelly-roll pan plus an 8-by-8-inch square pan. Baking times may vary slightly.

Makes about 40

Liliane Kaufmann insisted on different dinnerware for every weekend meal. Photograph by Rob Long.

GLOSSARY

Jane Citron

This glossary of cooking terms further explains the recipes in this book. We referred to the French classic, *Larousse Gastronomique* (*The Encyclopedia of Food, Wine Cookery* by Prosper Montagne); *Mastering the Art of French Cooking* by Julia Child, Simone Beck, and Louisette Bertholle; and *Cooking from A to Z* from the California Culinary Academy.

Ballontine: A rolled piece of meat or poultry filled with various ingredients. A ballontine is poached or low roasted and most often served at room temperature.

Baste: To spoon melted butter, fat, or liquid over foods.

Bain-Marie (Water Bath): A receptacle containing hot water in which sauces and dishes may be kept hot or cooked in a pan placed in the oven. Bain-marie, or water bath, is often used to cook fragile dishes that would disintegrate if cooked over direct heat.

Blanch: To plunge vegetables or other foods in boiling water until they have softened. Once softened, vegetables should be immersed in an ice water bath to stop cooking. Blanching most often refers to vegetables and allows them to be reheated without losing color.

Blind Baking of Pastry Crust, or Partially Baked: Blind baking a crust usually applies to dessert tarts and is done by lining the crust with foil and dried beans and baking until the crust is set (5 to 8 minutes) in a hot oven (check recipe). At this point, remove foil and beans, prick bottom of pastry with a fork and bake 8 to 10 minutes more.

Boil: The process of heating water to the boiling point (212 degrees F). Once the water reaches the boiling point, the temperature will not increase, but the water becomes more agitated and evaporates faster. Small bubbles on the surface work well for heating delicate sauces, stocks, and poaching. A *simmer* (continuous stream of small bubbles) is used for slow cooking. *Medium boil* provides more bubbles and heat, and a *rolling boil* with very active large bubbles, is good for cooking pasta, green vegetables, and reducing liquids.

Bouquet Garni: Aromatic herbs tied together into a little bundle. Parsley, thyme, and bay leaf are traditionally used and the proportion adjusted depending on the nature of the dish. The bouquets are removed from the dish before serving.

Braise: To brown foods in fat, then cook them in a covered casserole at a low to moderate temperature slowly with a small amount of liquid.

Caramelize: To cook sugar to a caramel degree by boiling sugar slowly with a small amount of water until mixture is amber in color. Caramel syrup is used to coat molds for custards and to make sauces and glazes.

Chiffonade: All plants and herbs, which are cut into fine strips or ribbons. Chiffonade most often applies to basil, lettuce, or sorrel. Cutting is best done by rolling leaves tightly then cutting into fine strips.

Coat: When a recipe calls for sauce to coat a spoon, it indicates how thick the sauce is. A sauce that coats the spoon is usually ready to use in a recipe.

Cooking in Oil: Sautéing, stir-frying, pan-frying, and deep-frying are different methods but all use fat. Sautéing uses a small amount, and the fat is often combined in the finished dish. Deep-fried foods are totally immersed in fat; the fat is never part of the finished dish. Both methods require high temperatures, which seal in flavor. To avoid greasy foods, closely monitor the temperature of the cooking fat. If the fat is too cool, the food will absorb too much fat. If the fat is too hot, the food burns, yet may remain undercooked inside. See also **Sauté.**

Cornichons: Small pickles, usually gherkins, which traditionally accompany pates and cold meats.

Daube: A French method for cooking meat. Meat is braised in stock, often with red wine enriched with various ingredients and seasoned with herbs.

Deglaze: After meat, chicken, or fish has been sautéed or roasted and the pan degreased (the cook should remove the excess fat from the pan), the liquid, usually wine or stock, is poured into the pan to capture all the coagulated juices. See also **Reduction** (both techniques are important in proper sauce making).

Dice: Cut vegetables or other foods into matchsticks approximately ⅛ inch wide, then cut the strips crosswise into small or medium dice.

Duxelle: Finely chopped mushrooms used in a variety of cooking preparations.

Farce: A forcement or stuffing. Latin in origin, farce is a French term.

Fold: To blend a delicate mixture, such as beaten egg whites, into a heavier mixture—most often a soufflé base—being careful not to break up or mash the egg whites or base.

Fraisage: Used in making pastry crusts, a fraisage is the finishing step to making the dough. Done with the heel of your hand, fraisage is a short pushing out of the dough, done twice to ensure an even blending of fat and flour.

Fromage Blanc: A French fresh curd cheese made from cow's milk similar to a refined version of American cottage cheese. Fromage Blanc is available at high-end supermarkets . Though the cheese may be eaten as is, Fromage Blanc makes a delicious cheesecake or Alsacienne Tarte.

Garlic: A bulb of garlic is called a *head;* a *clove* of garlic refers to the individual pieces of garlic that make up a head. Most recipes call for cloves and the parchment covering on a clove should be removed before using.

Haricots Verts: The French name for those wonderful small, slender green beans.

Heavy Cream: Heavy cream (sometimes called whipping cream) has more butterfat, which makes for better texture and richer flavor. Heavy cream is the best choice for desserts and the very best heavy cream is not ultra-pasteurized, which may provide longer shelf life but doesn't do much for flavor or texture. Though natural products are back in vogue it is often difficult to find "the real thing." Do the best you can but avoid creams marked "light."

Julienne: To cut vegetables or other foods into matchsticks approximately ⅛ inch wide.

Macerate and Marinate: To place foods in a liquid to absorb flavor or to tenderize. Macerate describes fruits and marinate refers to meats and usually calls for some kind of acid (wine, vinegar, lemon juice) with oil and seasonings.

Pate Brisee: A French pastry crust that may be used for savory or sweet dishes.

Persillade: Cooking term for chopped parsley often mixed with varying amounts of finely chopped garlic. In the Rack of Lamb Persillade recipe (page 122), olive oil and fresh bread crumbs are used as binding agents.

Pinch: As in "pinch of salt." A pinch is less than ¼ teaspoon, and it is added to a recipe with your fingers.

Poach: To cook an egg (or chicken) in a small amount of water. Remove the egg from the refrigerator, crack, and drop it on a small plate. In a frying pan, add enough water to cover the surface and bring it to a simmer. Gently slip the egg into the water. Eggs usually poach in 3 to 5 minutes. There are many ways to poach an egg. Some cooks add a little vinegar to the water, which helps lower the coagulation and speeds cooking. A truly fresh egg will have a thick, viscous white and round yolk that poaches into a plump, pretty round. To test for doneness in chicken, pierce the thickest part of the meat with a knife; the juices should run clear.

Pulse: The on-and-off or stop-and-start of the food processor. Pulsing controls how much the contents are processed.

Reduction: To boil down a liquid, reducing in quantity and concentrating its taste. See also **Deglaze.**

Sauté: From the French verb *saunter* which translates "to jump." In cooking, sauté is to brown food in hot fat—never crowding the pan—until it is cooked through or in preparation for a stew or casserole. It is important to be sure fat is hot enough, otherwise there will be no browning. Fat that is too hot will burn rather than cook. The food must be dry—moisture will create steaming. What you are cooking should making a sizzling sound as opposed to just lying inert in the pan.

Vinaigrette: The basic French dressing for salads and greens in France is a blend of good oil (usually extra-virgin olive oil), wine vinegar, salt, and freshly ground pepper. Other possible additions according to personal taste could be seasonal finely chopped herbs and genuine French Dijon mustard. The proportion of oil and vinegar is a personal decision ranging anywhere between 1 part vinegar to 4 parts oil. Our personal preference is 4 to 5 tablespoons oil to 1 tablespoon vinegar.

Whisk: Combining or beating ingredients by hand. Whisks come in all sizes. Choose one that is large enough but not too big and comfortable in your hand.

Zest: Zest is the colored portion of a citrus fruit, most often lemon, orange, or grapefruit. It may be cut into strips, fine threads, or finely grated. It is important to remove the bitter white pith when cutting or peeling the fruit.

SUGGESTED READING

This book is only an hors d'oeuvre. Here are some literary entrées and desserts we enjoyed and suggest you try:

Hagan, Bernardine. *Kentuck Knob: Frank Lloyd Wright's House for I. N. and Bernardine Hagan.* Pittsburgh: The Local History Co., 2005.

Hoffmann, Donald. *Frank Lloyd Wright's Fallingwater: The House and Its History.* New York: Dover Publications, Inc., 1978.

Hoffmann, Donald. *Frank Lloyd Wright's House on Kentuck Knob.* Pittsburgh: University of Pittsburgh Press, 2000.

Kaufmann, Edgar, jr. *Fallingwater: A Frank Lloyd Wright Country House.* New York: Abbeville Press Publishers, 1986.

Masters, Hilary. *Shadows on a Wall: Juan O'Gorman and the Mural in Patzcuaro.* Pittsburgh: University of Pittsburgh Press, 2005.

Sanderson, Arlene, ed. *Wright Sites: A Guide to Frank Lloyd Wright Public Places.* New York: Princeton Architectural Press, 2001.

Toker, Franklin. *Fallingwater Rising: Frank Lloyd Wright, E. J. Kaufmann, and America's Most Extraordinary House.* New York: Alfred A. Knopf, 2003.

Waggoner, Lynda S. *Fallingwater: Frank Lloyd Wright's Romance with Nature.* Fallingwater: Western Pennsylvania Conservancy, in association with Universe Publishing, 1996.

INDEX OF RECIPES

Notes: Page numbers in italics refer to illustrations. Seasonal menus appear at the end of the index. Each recipe is listed alphabetically and by category.

JANE AND BOB'S SEASONAL MENUS AT A GLANCE

Spring

SPRING LUNCHEON IN THE GARDEN, 114

Chilled Cucumber Bisque with Cheese Straws
Classic Salade Nicoise
Tomato and Roasted Red Pepper Tart
Daffodil Cake with Strawberry Compote and Whipped Cream

WELCOME SPRING DINNER, 121

Morel Mushroom Bisque
Roast Rack of Lamb Persillade
Zucchini Frite with Peppered Yogurt Sauce

Summer

COUNTRY BRUNCH, 125

Champagne Mimosas
Parmesan Cheese Straws
Muffin Basket (Banana Nut Muffins and
  Orange Poppy Seed Mini-Muffins)
Eggs Mornay
Sausage and Cheese Strata
Coffee Service and Cinnamon Palmiers

PICNIC IN THE WOODS, 130

Grilled Quail Wrapped in Pancetta
Shrimp Remoulade with Romaine and Radicchio "Slaw"
Orzo Summer Salad
Torte au Blette (Savory Spinach and Swiss Chard Bread Tort)
Chocolate Praline Bread Pudding
President Clinton's Cherry Raspberry Pie

The Fallingwater Cookbook was designed and typeset in Vendetta with Hypatia Sans display type by Kachergis Book Design of Pittsboro, North Carolina. It was printed on 80-pound Garda Silk White and bound by Friesens of Altona, Manitoba, Canada.